Early modern Duhallow, c.1534–1641

T0048990

Maynooth Studies in Local History

SERIES EDITOR Michael Potterton

This is one of six volumes in the Maynooth Studies in Local History series for 2022. It is also my first year as series editor, having taken over the role from the irreplaceable Raymond Gillespie, who held that position from 1995 to 2021, overseeing the publication of a veritable treasure trove of studies in those 27 years. Raymond established the series with Irish Academic Press as a direct result of the enormous success of the Maynooth MA in Local History programme, which began in 1992. Under Raymond's supervision, some 153 volumes were produced, authored by 140 different scholars (94 men and 46 women). The first volume, on education in nineteenth-century Meath, was written by Paul Connell, and the 153rd, on the Dublin Cattle Market in the 1950s and 1960s, was by Declan O'Brien. Eleven people have each contributed two volumes to the series, while Terry Dooley is the only person to have written three.

The remarkable collection now covers some 1,500 years of history across 31 counties, dealing variously with aspects of agriculture and fishing, architecture, crime and punishment, death and burial, economy and trade, education, famine, gender, healthcare, industry, language and literature, migration, music and the arts, politics, religion, society, travel and communication, urban development, war and much more besides. I am grateful to Raymond for entrusting the series to me, and to Four Courts Press for not vetoing the appointment. Together, I am sure that we can build on the sound foundations established over more than quarter of a century of diligent work.

The current crop of titles takes us from a broad look at religion and society in medieval Galway to a very specific and tragic event in Knockcroghery village on the night of 20 June 1921. En route we witness the gradual dismantling of Irish lordship in early modern north Co. Cork, and the development of nursing and midwifery in Co. Tipperary at the turn of the twentieth century. Finally, we have biographical sketches of two remarkable men of the nineteenth century – Thomas Conolly (1823–76) of Castletown House in Co. Kildare and botanist Nathaniel Colgan (1851–1919) of Dublin.

While the genesis and home of this series lie firmly at Maynooth, it is a mark of its appeal, its breadth and its inclusivity that this year's contributors are drawn from Carlow College, Glenstal Abbey, NUI Galway, Trinity College Dublin and the University of Limerick as well as Maynooth University.

Maynooth Studies in Local History: Number 156

Early modern Duhallow, c.1534–1641: the crisis, decline and fall of Irish lordship

David Heffernan

FOUR COURTS PRESS

Set in 11.5pt on 13.5pt Bembo by
Carrigboy Typesetting Services for
FOUR COURTS PRESS LTD
7 Malpas Street, Dublin 8, Ireland
www.fourcourtspress.ie
and in North America for
FOUR COURTS PRESS
c/o IPG, 814 N Franklin Street, Chicago, IL 60610

ISBN 978–1–80151–029–5

Printed in Ireland
by SprintPrint, Dublin

Contents

Note on conventions

The year is taken as beginning on 1 January, as opposed to 25 March, as was the convention in early modern Ireland owing to the retention of the Julian Calendar. Generally recognizable modern spellings have been used for personal names and place-names. Accordingly, Kanturk is referred to as such, rather than *Ceann Toirc*, and so forth. Throughout, the English community of Cork city and the other major towns are referred to as the Old English. The lordly families of English extraction such as the Roches who had adopted many of the political and social customs of their Irish neighbours are referred to as the Anglo-Irish.

Acknowledgments

The Covid-19 pandemic provided a window in which to research and write most of this book, the idea for which had been in the back of my head for several years. Opportunities arose to visit several research libraries in Dublin in autumn 2020 when such venues were briefly opened between waves of the virus. I would like to thank the staff of the National Library of Ireland, the Royal Irish Academy and the National Archives of Ireland for their assistance in providing material relating to the project during the rather straitened circumstances that prevailed at that time. The staff of Special Collections at University College Cork provided access by appointment in the autumn of 2020 as well, and without these visits it would not have been possible to finish the project at the time that I did. Finally, my thanks to Dr Michael Potterton for guiding the book through publication as the editor of the Maynooth Studies in Local History series and to Four Courts Press for publishing it.

Introduction

In the spring of 1580 the viceroy of Ireland, William Pelham, wrote to the Privy Council in England about Duhallow. He didn't know it though. Instead, Pelham referred to what Elizabethan officials termed 'the mountain of Sleulogher'. This region was, according to Pelham, a distinct area, sixteen miles (26km) wide and accounted to run fifty miles (80km) inland from the mouth of the River Feale south-east towards the Mullaghareirk Mountains in Duhallow. Thus, *Sliabh Luachra*, as we would term it today, covered much of north Co. Kerry, south-west Limerick and north-west Cork, encapsulating much of the barony of Duhallow around Rockchapel, Meelin and Newmarket. The area was largely impenetrable for the government in Pelham's time. Boggy and mountainous, it was impassable for crown forces for roughly ten months of the year. Such was the case in the spring of 1580. Days before his time of writing, Pelham's detachment had attempted to proceed north to Carrigafoyle Castle on the southern banks of the Shannon Estuary in their ongoing efforts to crush the rebellion of Gerald FitzGerald, fifteenth earl of Desmond. However, finding 'Sleulogher' impassable, they had sought a route across the River Feale near the sea. The operation went badly and nearly twenty men drowned before Pelham's forces made it through to Carrigafoyle.[1] Yet this would not be the last time that passage over 'the mountain of Sleulogher' proved a difficulty for crown forces in early modern Munster. At the height of the Nine Years War in 1600 the governor of Munster, Sir George Carew, would refer to the area being impassable owing to the wet weather.[2] Hence, Duhallow, dominated by the lordships of the MacDonogh-MacCarthys, the MacAuliffes, the O'Keeffes and the O'Callaghans, was an area of Ireland that was largely impervious to crown encroachments during the late sixteenth century. Yet by the mid-seventeenth century this had all changed. Extensive lands had come under the control of a cadre of New English landholders and the remnants of the Irish septs were experiencing dwindling political and economic fortunes. This book is a study of the Duhallow region during this tumultuous era and how the Irish lordships there experienced a crisis, decline and fall during the early modern period. Previous studies of early modern Duhallow have been limited. The region was afforded some attention by William Butler and Samuel McCarthy in their respective works on the MacCarthy kinship of Munster in the 1910s and 1920s.[3] McCarthy's work on sixteenth-century Duhallow, however, was limited to an internal rivalry within the MacDonogh lordship, while Butler's endeavours were marred by a reliance on an incredibly misleading article published by Herbert Webb Gillman in the 1890s.[4] Occasional research articles since have shed some considerable light on various aspects of the Duhallow lordships, chiefly the O'Callaghans.[5] Michael MacCarthy-Morrogh's magisterial study of the Munster Plantation from the 1580s down to the 1640s included a valuable account of the activities of Richard Aldworth and Philip Percival around Newmarket and Kanturk in the 1610s, 1620s and 1630s.[6] Most significantly, James Casey's meticulous doctoral thesis on 'Landownership in north Cork, 1584–1641', completed at UCC in 1988, dedicated a chapter to assessing the various land transfers that occurred throughout Duhallow during the reigns of Elizabeth I, James I and Charles I.[7] Nevertheless, a holistic study encompassing each of the four Duhallow lordships, the other sub-septs of the region, and their varying fortunes over the course of the Tudor and early Stuart periods is still wanting. What follows seeks to provide such a study.

If the lordships of the MacDonogh-MacCarthys, MacAuliffes, O'Callaghans and O'Keeffes have been relatively ignored it is because the story of these lordships is not one of intense resistance to crown encroachments followed by confiscation and plantation. This is what happened among the O'Connors and O'Mores of Laois and Offaly in the 1550s and 1560s, to the earls of Desmond in the 1570s and 1580s and to the O'Neills and O'Donnells in Ulster in the 1590s and 1600s. The plight of these septs, which terminated in the plantations of the midlands, Munster and Ulster, have long dominated the popular history of early modern Ireland. But there was another, more subtle conquest that occurred on just as great a scale in Ireland during the sixteenth and seventeenth centuries, one in which individual lordships were slowly worn down by an interventionist Tudor state

through increased crown taxation and legal intervention. Some
Irish lords opted to join periodic rebellions as a result of the crisis
wrought by this English governmental expansion. Others waited and
hoped they could prosper through accommodation of the Dublin
government. For many, however, crisis simply gave way to decline
and fall as deteriorating economic fortunes in the early seventeenth
century forced them to mortgage and sell their lands to New English
arrivistes. Finally, impoverished and embittered, many revolted in the
early 1640s when a new Irish insurrection burst forth from Ulster.
When that also failed, the fate of these lordships was sealed. This
alternative experience of conquest was just as critical to the death
of Gaelic Ireland as the more omnipresent conquest and plantation
experienced by the O'Neills and others. Duhallow in the early
modern period epitomizes this *other* conquest. Hence, what follows
is a narrative of how the lordships of the MacDonogh-MacCarthys,
MacAuliffes, O'Callaghans and O'Keeffes were gradually decimated
through a prolonged process of crisis, decline and fall.

1. Duhallow in Tudor times

The barony of Duhallow takes its name from the River Allow, which rises in the Mullaghareirk Mountains in the north-west of the region and flows east along the Cork–Limerick border, then south through Kanturk and finally joins the River Blackwater near Banteer in the south of Duhallow. On its western extremity, the barony borders county Kerry and is largely upland mountainous territory east towards Newmarket. Thereafter the barony gives way to more low-lying regions east towards where the barony terminates near Mallow. To the north lies Limerick, while the southern boundary is found near Millstreet and Aubane where it meets the baronies of Muskerry and Barretts. Curiously, in early modern times there were some overlapping jurisdictions and the Down Survey of the 1650s indicates that a pocket of land in the parish of Kilmeen in the south near Cullen formed part of county Kerry, despite being wholly surrounded by the baronial lands of Duhallow.[1]

At the time of the Kildare Rebellion in Ireland in 1534 Duhallow was dominated by four lordships.[2] Foremost was that of the MacDonogh-MacCarthys. The MacDonoghs had been pushed from their lands in Tipperary into Duhallow by the onslaught of the Cambro-Normans who conquered a great proportion of Ireland from the late twelfth century through to the fourteenth century. By Tudor times the MacDonoghs' landed presence was focused on the centre of Duhallow stretching in an arc from midway between Kanturk and Mallow, west to Kanturk and further south-west towards Cullen. The sept's principal seats were Kanturk Castle and Lohort Castle, with a significant stronghold also at Castle Cor.[3] Although the MacDonoghs were, from a military and landed perspective, on a relatively equal footing with the other septs of Duhallow, they nevertheless exercised lordship over the MacAuliffes, O'Keeffes and O'Callaghans. Hence the O'Callaghans were, for instance, expected to provide sixty cows annually as tribute to MacDonogh or 6s. 8d. in lieu of every cow, while they and the O'Keeffes and MacAuliffes

1. Kanturk Castle, Co. Cork, viewed from the north-west as it was constructed in the
early seventeeth century

were obliged to provide food and hospitality to MacDonogh and his
retinue when they passed through the sub-lords' lands.[4] This over-
lordship had multiple layers. Above the MacDonoghs the MacCarthy
Mór, the ostensible head of the Munster MacCarthys, reserved the
right to bestow the Munster lordships on the MacAuliffes, O'Keeffes
and O'Callaghans with a white wand. This may not have been purely
ceremonial and in 1579 we find Donal MacCarthy Mór anointing the
new O'Callaghan lord, Conor *na Cairrcce* (of the Rock). Additionally,
the MacCarthy Mór was entitled to have twenty-seven of his
galloglass mercenaries maintained by the three Duhallow sub-lords.[5]
Despite this role for the MacCarthy Mór, the MacDonoghs held a
position of pre-eminence within early modern Duhallow.[6]

The MacAuliffes occupied the greatest scope of land in the
region. Clanawley, as their territory was known, encompassed
much of the north and west of early modern Duhallow from
modern-day Newmarket north to the boundaries with Limerick
around Meelin and Rockchapel and west to the borders of county
Kerry. The southern boundary of Clanawley ran largely along the
course of the River Brogeen where the sept's lands met those of the
O'Keeffes.[7] Like the MacDonoghs, the MacAuliffes had been pushed

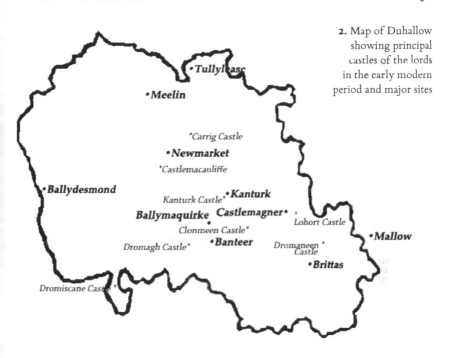

2. Map of Duhallow showing principal castles of the lords in the early modern period and major sites

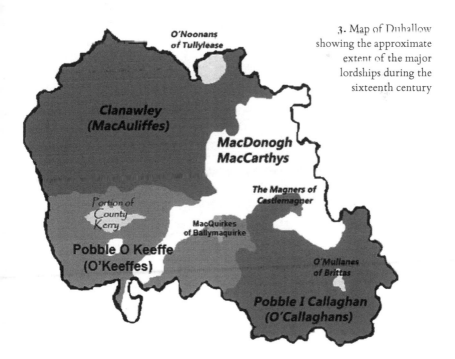

3. Map of Duhallow showing the approximate extent of the major lordships during the sixteenth century

into Duhallow in the late thirteenth and early fourteenth centuries owing to pressure from the Cambro-Norman newcomers. Their new home was comparatively unproductive land. Much of Clanawley was mountainous, boggy and heavily wooded. In particular the western parts of the lordship were largely poor, uninhabitable lands and it was this region that epitomized the impassable 'mountain of Sleulogher' reported on by English observers in Tudor times. Exactly how impenetrable this region was is best illustrated by the map of Britain and Ireland included in the 1572 edition of Abraham Ortelius's *Theatrum Orbis Terrarum* published at Antwerp. Here a large expanse of land stretching from central Duhallow west into county Kerry towards Tarbert is depicted as being entirely dominated by forests and mountains.[8] As such, even a European audience was aware in Elizabethan times that the MacAuliffe lands in western Duhallow were a mass of woodland and mountains. The eastern stretches of Clanawley were more habitable. Consequently, the political centre of the lordship was in the lands around *Áth Trasna*, literally meaning the crossing of the ford, in the region around Newmarket. Here approximately 1.5km to the south-west of the modern-day town was the clan's chief castle of Castle MacAuliffe, while about 5km to the north-east of that was the secondary castle of the lordship, Carrig Castle.[9] Clearly then, while the MacAuliffes held a considerable expanse of territory in the north and west of Duhallow, much of this was effectively waste land and their economic and political power was centralized in the regions around Newmarket.[10]

The O'Keeffes were the preponderant power in the south of Duhallow. Their territory, Pobble O Keeffe, was split into two blocks. One bordered county Kerry in the west and ran eastwards along the course of the River Blackwater through Cullen, where it encountered a strip of the MacDonogh lands running south towards Drishane. On the other side of this band the other section of the O'Keeffe lands ran north-east through Dromagh and Dromtarriff to around modern-day Banteer where it bordered the MacDonogh and O'Callaghan lordships.[11] A further block of land south of the Blackwater extended the O'Keeffes' territory to the southern extremity of the barony, however these lands were less accessible as the lowlands around the Blackwater gave way to the Boggeragh Mountains.[12] The sept had its principal castle at Dromagh just west of Banteer, with another major seat further to the south-west at Dromiscane Castle on the banks of the Blackwater between Millstreet and Cullen.[13] Prior to the incursions of the Cambro-Normans into Munster, the O'Keeffes were a major force around Fermoy, however they were pushed west into Duhallow in the thirteenth century before the arrival of the MacDonogh-MacCarthys, O'Callaghans and MacAuliffes owing to similar territorial pressure further to the north-east.[14] The arrival of the latter led to a border conflict that had residual implications and as late as the seventeenth century the MacAuliffes and the O'Keeffes were engaged in a dispute over a strip of land in western Duhallow.[15]

Finally, the east of the barony was dominated by the O'Callaghans. Pobble I Callaghan occupied a region encapsulating the modern-day parishes of Clonmeen and Kilshannig and the surrounding areas running from the region around Kanturk and Banteer further east along the course of the River Blackwater towards the eastern boundaries of the barony on the outskirts of Mallow. From there the lordship extended south towards the Boggeragh Mountains.[16] In this region a boundary dispute existed with the Barretts to the south-east who claimed suzerainty over seven quarters (approximately 840 acres) of land at Twoghie O'Murrehie.[17] Claiming descent from a tenth-century king of Cashel, the O'Callaghans had, like their neighbours in Duhallow, been pushed into the region during the fourteenth century, gradually cementing their position along the Blackwater west of Mallow between the 1360s and 1420s.[18] The chief seat of the sept in the sixteenth century was at Dromaneen Castle on the banks of the Blackwater, while Clonmeen was also a substantial seat about 10km further upriver.[19] A third important castle was at Dromore at the eastern extremity of the lordship, most likely built as a strategic military castle on the borders of the sept's territory.[20] At the outset of the Tudor intervention in Ireland, the O'Callaghans occupied a strategic position along the River Blackwater and in proximity to the main fording point thereof at Mallow, while their lands stretching west to Kanturk were relatively good agricultural land by comparison with their neighbours further to the west in 'the mountain of Sleulogher'.

Beyond the major septs there were few landholders in the lordship of Duhallow. Much of the land in Clanawley, Pobble O Keeffe and Pobble I Callaghan was held by different branches of the MacAuliffes, O'Keeffes and O'Callaghans. Extensive areas of this land could be periodically redistributed among the members of the sept, typically upon the accession of a new lord, while other sections were held on a more concrete basis by collateral branches.[21] One of the few exceptions was in the south of the barony where the MacQuirkes, a scion of the O'Keeffes, held approximately nine ploughlands at Ballymaquirke between Banteer and Kanturk.[22] The O'Callaghans had a near neighbour west of Mallow in the O'Mullanes who had a significant presence around Brittas.[23] Another notable contingency were the O'Noonans, the coarbs of the ecclesiastical lands of Tullylease at the northern extremity of the barony. These hereditary religious officers administered a property of nearly one thousand acres, which was a geographically removed parcel of the Augustinian priory of Kells in Ossory.[24] The presence of the Anglo-Irish, the descendants of the many Anglo-Norman families which had conquered much of Ireland during the twelfth and thirteenth centuries, was limited in the lordship. Only the Magners of Castlemagner east of Kanturk had any major holdings.[25]

The military forces available to the Duhallow lords were considerable. A treatise of the mid-1550s describes MacDonogh-MacCarthy as being able to muster two dozen horsemen, at least sixty galloglass or mercenaries, and one hundred kern or Irish infantry troops, while O'Keeffe was allegedly able to bring a dozen horsemen and one hundred kern into the field.[26] A separate 'Book' on the reformation of Ireland written in 1574 by the former governor of Munster, Humphrey Gilbert, stated that O'Callaghan and MacAuliffe each had one hundred kern and twelve and eight horsemen respectively.[27] However, towards the end of the Tudor period George Carew suggested that MacAuliffe had upwards of eighty cavalry at his disposal and it may have been the case that this particular Duhallow lord had an unusual number of horsemen in his service the better to traverse the mountainous inclines of Clanawley.[28] Therefore, even allowing for some exaggeration by Tudor observers about the militarized state of Ireland, it seems clear that the Duhallow lords had a considerable retinue of military forces at their disposal during the sixteenth century. Consequently, it is unsurprising to learn that the MacAuliffes were able to win a 'great battle' over the Munster FitzGeralds in 1535 as recorded in the Annals of the Four Masters.[29]

Previous studies of early modern Duhallow have almost entirely overlooked the population of the region below the ruling lineages.[30]

The Tudor fiants – records of warrants, pardons and other legal documents issued during the sixteenth century – reveal much about the population of Duhallow.[31] For instance, by the zenith of the reign of Elizabeth I there was a concentration of individuals at Castlemacauliffe near modern-day Newmarket, foremost among which were the O'Shines or O'Sheas. In 1601 there were five adult males of this lineage listed at the MacAuliffe settlement, while the presence of some O'Donoghues, O'Learys, O'Murchus, MacDonoghs and O'Sheehans here suggests that in addition to being a centre of MacAuliffe political power Castlemacauliffe was also a considerable economic hub.[32] Slightly to the north-east at Carrig Castle the MacAuliffes' secondary centre of power had a smaller settlement inhabited by several O'Scanlans.[33] At Castle Cor between Lohort and Liscarroll there were numerous O'Cormics and O'Sullivans recorded in the 1570s.[34] Various other surnames appear with the same frequency as the O'Shines at Castlemacauliffe. Foremost were the O'Flynns. The surname abounds at the main settlement sites along the River Blackwater in Pobble I Callaghan, notably Clonmeen and Dromaneen.[35] However, none were as numerous as the O'Connells, members of which surname group were living in significant numbers at sites such as Rossline about 3km east of Castlemacauliffe, at Meelaherragh near Kanturk, north of that at Clonrobin and also further to the north-east at Ballybahallagh just to the south-west of Liscarroll on the Duhallow side of the baronial boundary.[36]

We have little direct information with which to establish the economic circumstances that obtained in Duhallow during the sixteenth century. However, the nature of the terrain and the heavy expanses of woodland across much of the region would have promoted a considerable reliance on pastoral rather than agrarian farming. Cows and other livestock would have been central to economic life, as exemplified in the tribute of sixty cows which the O'Callaghans provided annually to the MacDonoghs. Equally, the prevalence of the land unit *gniomh* (the grass of one cow) in the Duhallow region and the fossilization of 'Gneeves' in local place-names is reflective of the reliance on pastoral farming in the uplands of western Duhallow.[37] However, this is not to suggest that arable farming was not practised in north-west Cork. Eve Campbell's recent fine study of the landscape of the O'Callaghan territory demonstrates that at least nine townlands in that lordship had place-names including the element *gort* (arable field), a clear indication that arable farming was being practised to a considerable degree in eastern Duhallow in Tudor times.[38] Even here though in the low-lying, more productive lands along the Blackwater mixed agriculture was practised and the O'Callaghans almost certainly engaged in booleying in the south-east of Duhallow where they took their cattle for summer pasture on the slopes of the Boggeragh Mountains.[39] Finally, the heavily forested portions of the barony were well-regarded for the timber they could provide. By the early 1590s the Mallow-based planter, Thomas Norris, had an arrangement with the O'Callaghans to acquire timber from their lands. This understanding was expanded by the future first earl of Cork, Sir Richard Boyle, in the early seventeenth century as he sought to acquire extensive timber for his many ironworks throughout Munster.[40]

There is minimal evidence with which to speculate on how extensive the villages of Tudor Duhallow were and what the commercial significance of them might have been. Clearly such urbanization as there was would have occurred in the central corridor of the barony in the low-lying region through which the River Blackwater and the River Allow flowed west towards Mallow. This area encompassed the political centres of the four lordships at Castlemacauliffe, Carrig Castle, Kanturk, Lohort, Dromagh, Dromaneen and Clonmeen. We have already seen that there was a significant settlement around the MacAuliffe stronghold of Castlemacauliffe. The evidence is even more substantive for Kanturk. During the reign of Elizabeth I a large concentration of individuals were living either at Kanturk or very near to it at Clonrobin and Corbally not far to the north of the modern-day town. These included numerous MacSweeneys, MacEgans, O'Komans, O'Scullys, O'Regans, O'Keeffes, Gibbons, O'Connells, and of course the MacDonoghs themselves.[41] Furthermore, a fiant of 1573 lists a David O'Fihely of Kanturk as a merchant, indicating that the primary MacDonogh stronghold had developed a significant economic function.[42] Similarly, there is evidence to suggest that Clonmeen was developing as a centre of some trade within Pobble I Callaghan.[43] All of this is not to say that sites such as Castlemacauliffe, Kanturk and Clonmeen were market-towns in the English sense, but these were clearly sites of some concentrated settlement by the sixteenth century with a modicum of economic activity and trade occurring thereat.

Irish society in Duhallow would have reflected the class structure found elsewhere in Ireland. At the top were the lords themselves and the members of their lineages. Next to them were the retainers and learned classes such as the brehons, bards and medical professionals. Prominent among these were the esteemed O'Dalys, which patronymic appears twice among lists of residents at the O'Callaghan settlement at Clonmeen in the late sixteenth century.[44] Perhaps more important were the MacEgans, hereditary bards to the MacDonogh-MacCarthys, who held lands at Corbally on the north-eastern outskirts of Kanturk and further to the east at Ballygrady.[45] This tier would also have included prominent mercenary lineages such as the MacSweeneys, a major galloglass sept associated with the MacCarthy Mórs of wider Munster who by the sixteenth century had acquired lands at Ballintober between Kanturk and Castlemagner, and also further to the west around Derrynatubbrid and Derrygalun near modern-day Boherbue.[46] Below these learned classes were the landholders who held from the ruling lineage of the lordship. What information we have available for the lordships of Duhallow in the sixteenth century indicates that many of these were in fact collateral branches of the sept. Accordingly, in the 1590s the freeholders in Pobble I Callaghan were nearly uniformly other O'Callaghans.[47] Finally, the lower rung of Irish society in the lordships of Duhallow would have consisted of landless churls or labourers.[48] Hierarchically, these different tiers were interconnected through a complex series of obligations to provide entertainment, hospitality and foodstuffs, often to support the lords' military retinues. These Gaelic exactions such as 'coign and livery', 'soren' and 'bonnaught' prevailed throughout the greater part of Gaelic Ireland, and despite the aspersions cast on them by English observers were not greatly onerous to the commons, who were not tied to the land and were free to negotiate better terms as tenants elsewhere.[49] This was owing to the considerably under-populated state of the country during the sixteenth century and any lord's power was measured according to the number of people he could retain on his lands, rather than the sheer quantity of land itself. This placed the commons in an advantageous position and the bishop of Cork, Cloyne and Ross proclaimed in 1596 that the common people often 'continue not past three years in a place', doubtlessly moving regularly to avail of better terms elsewhere.[50] Unfortunately, though, our information for these lower orders in early modern Duhallow is disappointingly limited.

These latter constraints aside, it appears in the early years of the sixteenth century to have reflected the pattern of Irish lordship elsewhere in the country. Internal rivalries within lordships could proliferate. For instance, a struggle for control over the MacDonogh-MacCarthys between two closely related branches of the family arose in the 1540s and continued to have serious and growing implications for the lordship down to the end of the Tudor period.[51] Equally, external conflicts arose which led to seasonal military campaigns. In 1510 Gerald FitzGerald, eighth earl of Kildare, with an army of allies including the O'Donnells of Ulster, campaigned into Munster against the Desmond Geraldines and their affinity in the south. In the course of this campaign Kanturk was plundered and the MacDonoghs were drawn into the conflict.[52] In response to a 'predatory incursion' into Duhallow by Conor O'Connor Kerry in 1524, Cormac Óge MacDonogh retaliated in a campaign that led to the wounding and imprisonment of O'Connor Kerry.[53] There is, though, little evidence to suggest that these campaigns developed into enduring or intense regional conflicts. Rather they fit the pattern of Irish warfare in the early sixteenth century, being low in intensity and often taking the shape of cattle raiding with limited casualties.[54] In this respect, a political equilibrium obtained in Duhallow during the early part of the reign of Henry VIII (1509–47). But this was about to change. In the latter part of Henry's reign a dramatic shift in the Tudor approach to Ireland occurred. The repercussions of that shift were to reverberate in regions such as Duhallow for the entirety of the early modern period.

2. Duhallow and the re-emergence of crown power in Tudor Munster, c.1534–79

Historians have long viewed the rebellion in 1534 of Thomas FitzGerald, tenth earl of Kildare, or Silken Thomas, as a major turning point in Irish history.[1] This is wholly understandable. When FitzGerald rebelled in 1534 it set in motion events that initiated the Tudor conquest of Ireland. The abortive rebellion was crushed in 1535. Within months officials in Dublin were evaluating the best way to expand crown rule into those parts of Leinster immediately adjoining the Pale. In the mid-1540s this led to a military incursion into the midlands lordships of the O'Connors and O'Mores in Laois and Offaly which in the 1550s morphed into a state-run plantation of the midlands. Drives north into east Ulster and further westwards towards the Shannon accompanied these shifts, while from the 1530s efforts were underway to re-impose some semblance of royal power in Munster and Connacht.[2] Admittedly there were periodic efforts to reinvigorate crown rule in the south prior to the 1530s. The second earl of Surrey, Thomas Howard, had been sent to Ireland in 1520 with a view to reforming the country and this early initiative had some bearing on Munster. There was, for instance, talk of bringing the earldom of Desmond back into the crown fold from the position of alienation that had developed between the Munster FitzGeralds and the crown since the execution of the eighth earl of Desmond, Thomas FitzGerald, in 1468.[3] Subtle indications of future incursions into the Duhallow region by the crown were seen when Surrey entered negotiations with the Carbery branch of the MacCarthys to begin holding their lands from Henry VIII under English tenure, right on the southern periphery of Duhallow.[4] Yet these efforts were transient and it was only from the mid-1530s that consequential reform efforts were undertaken. It is to this period that the origins of the crisis of the Irish lordships of Duhallow can ultimately be traced.

The internal leadership of the Duhallow lordships from the 1530s through to the reign of Elizabeth I (1558–1603) present wildly contrasting examples of stability and instability. The situation in the sub-lordships was one in which strong rulers held power for decades and in the mid-Elizabethan period succeeded in passing on their estates unhindered to their sons. The epitome of this continuity was surely to be found among the O'Keeffes. In 1525 Art MacDaniel O'Keeffe succeeded his father as head of the O'Keeffe *oireacht* (territory or lordship). The new lord was most likely just 20 or so years of age at the time of his succession and would rule Pobble O Keeffe for nearly six decades through to his death in 1583.[5] On that latter occasion he was succeeded by his son Art Óge O'Keeffe who in turn ruled for some thirty-plus years into the mid-to-late 1610s.[6] The O'Keeffe lordship consequently enjoyed a stable and unbroken line of two long-lived rulers between the early sixteenth and early seventeenth centuries. Similarly, in Pobble I Callaghan when the head of the sept, Teige Roe O'Callaghan, died around 1537 he was succeeded by his son Donogh MacTeige.[7] Donogh was to provide forty years of unbroken leadership down to his own death in 1577 or early 1578. His long reign was celebrated in the anonymous bardic poem *Deacair comhaireamh a chreach* ('Difficult it is to enumerate his spoilings'), which glorified the O'Callaghan lord's exploits in conducting scores of raids throughout Munster.[8] A swift change of leadership occurred following his death. Donogh's grandson Callaghan MacConor briefly held power before his premature death by drowning in the River Blackwater just months later in 1578.[9] Control of Pobble I Callaghan consequently passed to another branch of the sept, the O'Callaghans of the Prior (a branch who acquired their name through their association with the priory of Ballybeg near Buttevant), with Conor *na Cairrce* (of the Rock) O'Callaghan, a grandson of Teige Roe O'Callaghan (d. 1537), assuming the chieftainship in 1578. As with Donogh MacTeige, Conor's reign would prove long-lived and despite some internal challenges he ruled the lordship for three-and-a-half decades until his death in 1612.[10] Though the succession of the MacAuliffe lordship through the sixteenth century is less clear, it seems that here too a long-lived ruler, Melaghlin MacDermot MacAuliffe, exercised control over Clanawley for many years prior to his eventual death in 1579.[11] Thus, the three sub-lordships of Duhallow were ruled with a remarkable degree of continuity by long-lived rulers, Art MacDaniel O'Keeffe, Donogh MacTeige O'Callaghan and Melaghlin MacDermot MacAuliffe, for the vast majority of the period between the 1530s and the outbreak of the Desmond Rebellion in 1579. The situation could not have been more different among the MacDonoghs. A bitter dispute between two branches of the sept raged across the entirety of the sixteenth century. This had its roots in the death in 1501 of Donogh MacDonogh-MacCarthy, seventh lord of Duhallow. Donogh was survived by at least two sons, Cormac and Owen, the elder of whom, Cormac, succeeded in 1501 as eighth lord of the MacDonoghs.[12] Cormac ruled for forty years, but the surviving evidence, much of it written in the context of a bitter succession dispute in the 1580s and 1590s, suggests that he was then murdered by his brother Owen in 1541 who usurped the lordship as ninth lord of Duhallow.[13] What followed was sixty years of rivalry between the descendants of Cormac and Owen. During this, several members of each branch were murdered by the other, leading to a rapid turnover of leadership throughout the 1540s, 1550s, 1560s and 1570s. Such was the scale of this that the rivals for the lordship in the 1580s and 1590s, Donogh MacCormac and Dermot MacOwen, were the seventeenth and eighteenth lords of the MacDonoghs respectively, indicating ten changes of leadership between 1541 and the early 1590s.[14]

It was within this mixture of political instability among the MacDonoghs, but contrastingly stable leadership within the O'Keeffe, O'Callaghan and MacAuliffe lordships, that the changes which characterized sixteenth-century Duhallow occurred. Those changes and the crisis that they wrought were intrinsically connected down to the 1580s with the Tudor government's relationship with the earls of Desmond. The first signs of this link were seen in 1539. In the late 1530s the Tudor regime had elected to favour the suit of James FitzMaurice as earl of Desmond over the de-facto thirteenth earl, James FitzJohn.[15] Pursuant from this, in mid-1539 FitzMaurice arrived in Munster to press his claim militarily and in November the lord deputy, Leonard Grey, went southwards to support him with a crown army. Entering Duhallow, the crown's army camped near Dromaneen Castle in Donogh MacTeige O'Callaghan's country for four days, during which time Desmond appeared on the other side of the Blackwater to signal his continuing defiance.[16] This action, with its incursion of a crown army into Duhallow to intervene in the politics of Munster, was a harbinger of things to come. For the next forty-five years the lordships of north-west Cork would experience increasing volatility owing to their relationships with forces outside of Duhallow itself, above all the Tudor regime and the earldom of Desmond.

In the short term, however, the unrest of the late 1530s proved ephemeral. Just months after Grey's incursion into Pobble I Callaghan the government's favoured candidate to replace Desmond, James FitzMaurice, was killed near Fermoy. The administration in Dublin then quickly reached an accommodation with James FitzJohn who was recognized in his position as earl of Desmond.[17] This was in line with the rolling out of a more conciliatory approach to government in Ireland under the newly appointed viceroy, Sir Anthony St Leger. From his appointment in the summer of 1540, St Leger was concerned above all to keep expenditure in Ireland at a minimum.[18] Consequently, during the early 1540s St Leger embarked on a new programme of government in Ireland, one which eschewed costly military campaigns and instead sought to pacify the Irish lordships through a programme of anglicization. Accordingly in 1541 an Act for the Kingly Title was passed through the Dublin parliament elevating Henry VIII from his previous position as lord of Ireland to that of king of Ireland. In tandem, an initiative to have the Irish lords surrender their lands and receive them back from the king with English titles was initiated. The marquee ennoblement was Conn O'Neill who in 1542 was made first earl of Tyrone, while in Duhallow Murrough O'Brien became the first earl of Thomond. Although it proved abortive, the concept of having Irish lords surrender their lands and having them regranted from the crown, or 'surrender and regrant' as it became known, would have implications for the Duhallow lordships for decades to come.[19]

In the shorter term, St Leger's reforms of the early 1540s led to the first formal agreement between the Tudor regime and some Duhallow lords. In 1542 the viceroy brought an army of four hundred troops into Munster to campaign against Donal MacCarthy Mór and his allies. This show of force resulted in an accord being concluded between the antagonists in the late autumn of 1542.[20] This agreement was reached between St Leger, the earl of Desmond, the under-treasurer William Brabazon, the master of the ordnance John Travers and the marshal Osborn Etchingham on the government's side, and on the other side the lords Barry and Roche, MacCarthy Mór, MacCarthy Reagh, Teige MacCormac MacCarthy Lord of Muskerry, O'Sullivan Beare, and from Duhallow Donogh O'Callaghan and one Owen MacDonogh, who it seems had just recently murdered his brother, the eighth lord of Duhallow, Cormac MacDonogh. By the terms of this the Munster lords would acknowledge Henry VIII as their king. The Duhallow lords and their neighbours would not receive English titles in the same way O'Neill and O'Brien recently had, but the indenture they agreed to in the autumn of 1542 was a clear recognition of Henry's promulgation as king of Ireland the previous year. Further stipulations of the 1542 indenture included a prohibition on exacting black rents from the port towns of Munster, while there was also a hint here of the introduction of wider crown taxation throughout the province. But the major significance lay in a stipulation that a council of arbitration would be established in Munster to adjudicate on matters of contention between these Irish and Anglo-Irish lords. This would consist of the earl of Desmond and the three bishops of Cork, Waterford and Ross. Should any one lord raid the lands of another the matter would be adjudicated on by the quorum. Moreover, power was also granted to Desmond and the three bishops along with several other south-Munster officials to issue decrees, which the lords, including MacDonogh and O'Callaghan, were expected to abide by.[21]

The 1542 indenture presaged the drive towards greater administrative oversight of Munster by the English government in Dublin that would ensue over the following forty years. Successive administrations in the final years of the reign of Henry VIII and those of his children, Edward VI (1547–53), Mary I (1553–8) and Elizabeth I (1558–1603), were anxious that the lordships of Munster should be brought to conform more closely to English political, social and economic practices.[22] To this end it was envisaged that lordships such as those of the MacDonoghs, O'Callaghans, O'Keeffes and MacAuliffes would be directed or coerced into introducing succession by *primogeniture* according to English practice, to establish freeholders on their lands, and to forego using the system of Irish exactions such as 'coign and livery' in favour of English forms of taxation.

Moreover, English administrators were particularly anxious that the Brehon law ought to be replaced with the English common law. The method increasingly favoured to effect these changes throughout the 1540s and 1550s was to establish a provincial council in Munster. Such bodies had been advocated for in Ireland since the early 1530s.[23] Indeed, the 1542 indenture was in many respects a pseudo-council, with its strictures of oversight in regions such as the lands of the MacDonoghs and Pobble I Callaghan.

Plans for more formal councils, in many instances headed by presidents, abounded into the later 1540s and 1550s. These were primarily originating among senior officials in the Dublin administration, notably the lord chancellor of the 1540s, John Alen, and the master of the ordnance, John Travers.[24] Such designs were very nearly realized in 1546 when the regime in London sent a directive to Ireland for a Munster council to be established at Limerick headed by the archbishop of Cashel, Edmund Butler.[25] This particular scheme was stillborn owing to the death of Henry VIII just months later in 1547.[26] Nevertheless, proposals for a Munster council continued through the late 1540s and into the 1550s from high and middle-ranking officials in Ireland such as the solicitor general and surveyor, Walter Cowley, and the muster official, Thomas Walshe.[27] The latter individual composed an extensive treatise in 1552 outlining the most detailed proposal of this kind. The potential implications for Duhallow and its lordships were vast. Walshe envisaged that this council and its president should be responsible for no less than the examination of all land titles in Munster to establish proper ownership according to English property conventions. This not only threatened to erode the basis of lordship in Duhallow, where land was held jointly by the sept and changed hands according to the political circumstances of the day, but a further proposition by Walshe to convert the Irish system of exactions into a myriad array of English crown taxations would, if accomplished, wholly diminish the economic and political power of the Duhallow lords. Moreover, the president and council would be backed with the threat of military force, accompanied throughout the province by a force of one hundred men. These would reside periodically at different towns throughout Munster where gaols and courts would be established, the nearest to Duhallow being at Kilmallock just to the north-east of the barony over the Limerick border. Proposals such as Walshe's, with its emphasis on the replacement of Irish lordship with English provincial government, augured ill for the lords of Duhallow.[28] And yet no president and council materialized as efforts to do so were constantly scuppered during the 1550s and into the early 1560s. In the interim, events in the south and for the Duhallow lords often continued as before, with the MacDonoghs, O'Callaghans, O'Keeffes and MacAuliffes enjoying a large degree of non-interference in their affairs. There is markedly little available evidence for events within Duhallow in the mid-sixteenth century, but from the mid-1560s onwards we get a greater glimpse of occurrences in north-west Cork. The barony's position as part of the wider Irish milieu of Munster and the midlands during the 1560s is exemplified in the movements of Cormac MacBrian O'Connor at this time. A son and the political heir of the former lord of Offaly, Brian O'Connor Faly, Cormac had been intermittently involved in rebellions against the crown in the midlands throughout the late 1550s and 1560s. At some point in late 1566 or early 1567 he was in Munster where he consulted with the earl of Desmond. There his brother Cahir caught up with Cormac near Adare in Limerick before they proceeded south into Duhallow. Over the space of two weeks the brothers visited the MacAuliffe lands, Pobble O Keeffe, MacDonogh's country and several senior members of the O'Callaghans.[29] We have a frustrating dearth of information as to what might have been the purpose of this tour of Duhallow, but given Cormac's position as a perennial rebel in the midlands it is plausible that O'Connor was attempting to build support in Munster for a new insurrection against the midlands plantation in Laois and Offaly. His re-entry into rebellion soon afterwards would certainly favour this interpretation.

More obvious signs of the Duhallow lords' continuing engagement with the factions of Gaelic Ireland are seen in the two major battles between private lords which occurred in Munster in the mid-to-late 1560s. The first of these is the more infamous. On 8 February 1565 a clash occurred between the forces and allies of Gerald FitzGerald, fifteenth earl of Desmond, and Thomas Butler, tenth earl of Ormond, at Affane in west Waterford. For years tensions had been brewing between the two senior Munster lords over competing land claims and the rights to the lucrative prise wines in the ports of

Youghal and Kinsale. Now in the early spring of 1565 this boiled over into outright conflict. At the resulting battle, the lords of Duhallow played a substantial part. Desmond later testified that his forces had included those of the MacDonoghs and the MacAuliffes, while the O'Callaghans had been represented by a Dermot O'Callaghan and his son Dermot Óge.[30] The encounter resulted in Desmond's incarceration by Ormond at Waterford, following which both earls were summoned to London.[31] Affane initiated a period of nearly a decade in which Desmond spent most of his time imprisoned in either London or Dublin. It was during this period of detention that the second major battle involving the Duhallow lords occurred in Munster, this at Lixnaw in the summer of 1568. The conflict on this occasion was between Thomas FitzMaurice, sixteenth Lord of Lixnaw, and the forces of James FitzMaurice, a near cousin of the earl of Desmond and the preponderant power in south Munster during the earl's incarceration in London. On this occasion Teige Roe O'Callaghan was involved among James FitzMaurice's followers.[32] Indeed the Duhallow lords were engaging in widespread military activity in 1568. Just weeks after the hostilities at Lixnaw, Donal MacCarthy Mór, with a force including the MacDonoghs, O'Keeffes and MacAuliffes, plundered the lands of the Roches around Fermoy to the east of Duhallow, seizing 1,500 cattle, 100 horse and 7,000 sheep.[33]

The continuing independence of a great many of the lords of Munster, those in Duhallow included, of which the conflicts at Affane and Lixnaw were symptomatic, had not escaped the attention of crown officials. With plans for a provincial council perpetually stalling, a number of individuals had turned to the idea of establishing colonies in Munster as a means of pacifying the region. One such effort involved an attempted land-grab by Peter Carew. Based on often specious claims to territories owing to their having allegedly been held by his ancestors centuries earlier, Carew was aggressively pressing such claims in south Munster, Carlow and Meath in the late 1560s.[34] At one point the lands of the MacDonoghs in Duhallow were targeted, but these particular claims were not advanced in any substantive fashion.[35] Others though were much more determined. It has long been known through the work of Nicholas Canny that the late 1560s saw the emergence of numerous initiatives among English officials in England and Ireland to colonize sections of east

Ulster and southern Munster.[36] Generally these schemes focused on the coastlines. Such endeavours were led by a cohort of individuals among whom Humphrey Gilbert and Warham St Leger, son of the earlier viceroy of Ireland, were the most prominent. Although their designs are relatively well known, the focus when examining Gilbert, St Leger and their associates' proposals on establishing coastal colonies at sites such as Baltimore and Bearhaven has led scholars to elide the significant territorial ambitions they had further inland. These included Duhallow. In a series of petitions which they addressed to the Privy Council in England in 1568 and 1569 these aspiring planters effectively sought the lands of the entire wider MacCarthy affinity in south Munster, including the MacDonogh-MacCarthy lordship of Duhallow and the lordship of Pobble I Callaghan. The lands of the MacAuliffes and the O'Keeffes were not sought and the initiative did not materialize at this time. However, in petitioning to be granted a wide extent of land stretching from the Limerick border south to the Boggeragh Mountains and from Kanturk east to Mallow, this company of adventurers opened up for the first time under the Tudors the possibility of a plantation of much of Duhallow.[37]

These plans for a widespread plantation of Munster actually appear to have been green-lit in the spring of 1569.[38] Yet they were not realized. Just weeks later, rebellions erupted across much of Ireland. The foremost of these in Munster was led by James FitzMaurice, Desmond's cousin and the de facto leader of the Munster Geraldines during the earl's detention in England. A zealous Catholic, FitzMaurice entertained hopes of overthrowing Tudor rule in Ireland and offering the kingdom to a member of the House of Habsburg to be selected with the assent of Philip II of Spain and the Vatican.[39] Now in the summer of 1569 he attempted to further these aims by initiating a rebellion. The ensuing insurrection would last down to 1573, though the most active phase was over by 1571.[40] The impact of the rebellion on Duhallow and its lords was largely restricted to the early part of the war. Both Warham St Leger and Patrick Sherlock, a senior servant of the earl of Ormond, had indicated as early as February 1569 that MacDonogh's loyalty to the crown was very doubtful should any unrest arise, while Sherlock also suggested that Art O'Keeffe and Donogh MacTeige O'Callaghan were strong adherents of the earl of Clancar and MacDonogh.[41] It is frustratingly unclear exactly which MacDonogh lord was involved here. Those who reported on his joining the rebellion and submission later in 1569 followed the general convention for English officials in the 1560s and 1570s when remarking on the lords of Duhallow of simply calling them MacDonogh, MacAuliffe, O'Keeffe and O'Callaghan without providing a first name. Such was the level of turnover of lords within the MacDonogh lordship in the early Elizabethan period that it is not wholly clear which lord was preponderant there in 1569. Whoever was the MacDonogh lord of the late 1560s, St Leger and Sherlock were wholly correct in doubting his fidelity. No sooner had FitzMaurice entered rebellion than MacDonogh joined him along with Clancar. So too did Melaghlin MacAuliffe and Art O'Keeffe.[42] The O'Callaghans of the Prior were also certainly involved among the rebels too, though there appears to have been no direct implication of Donogh MacTeige O'Callaghan in the summer of 1569.[43] In June MacDonogh was involved with his troops in the first major action of the war, the destruction of the colony that St Leger and Richard Grenville had erected at Kerrycurrihy south of Cork city.

MacDonogh's involvement in the rebellion was to prove short-lived, while the MacAuliffes and O'Keeffes were speedily brought to surrender. In the early autumn the lord deputy Sir Henry Sidney campaigned south into Cork, gathering support from the loyalist Barrys and Roches around Fermoy before proceeding to Cork city. Sidney then headed north-west to Duhallow. This was likely the single greatest show of military power by an English army within the confines of Duhallow to date under the Tudors. Entering Pobble I Callaghan, Sidney had Donogh MacTeige temporarily surrender the O'Callaghans' major castles to ensure the sept's continuing loyalty, before passing further west into the lands of the MacDonoghs where he later claimed that he had 'won and pulled down castles, burned and spoiled villages and fields'.[44] There may have been a touch of hyperbole here, but it does suggest that Sidney had used scorched earth or the burning of crops in Duhallow in 1569. As a result, Melaghlin MacAuliffe and Art O'Keeffe surrendered in the early autumn just weeks after the initiation of the campaign.[45] Sidney departed Munster at that juncture, leaving Humphrey Gilbert to oversee the war effort as military governor of the province. At roughly the same time the earl of Ormond campaigned through south Limerick, north-west Cork and north Kerry, seizing several rebel castles. During this military action he captured and placed a crown ward in a fort which he referred to as 'Portetrynawde' on the mountain of Sliabh Luachra.[46] This was almost certainly the old Geraldine castle of *Phort Trí Namhad* (fort of the three enemies) or Portrinard some 2km north of Abbeyfeale along the banks of the River Feale in south-west Limerick.[47] Lying just 10km from the edges of the MacAuliffe lands in Clanawley, this brought a standing crown garrison into the heart of the mountainous region of Sliabh Luachra in a manner that had not previously been attempted by the crown. As such, with his lands having been ravaged by Sidney and a fort now garrisoned with crown troops just over the Limerick border from Duhallow, MacDonogh resigned himself to seeking terms with the crown. On 6 December he appeared before the governor at Limerick and submitted to the queen's mercy.[48] Thus ended the involvement of the Duhallow lords in FitzMaurice's rebellion.

The early 1570s did not bring any respite to the increasing intervention of Tudor government into Munster. Late in 1570 Sir John Perrot was finally appointed as the first president of the province. In the short term, Perrot was charged with completing the mopping-up operations to bring FitzMaurice's rebellion to a full conclusion. Lords such as MacDonogh and Art O'Keeffe were involved in aiding the crown in these endeavours.[49] In the long run, Perrot's appointment initiated a period of increased administrative oversight. For instance, in the early summer of 1573 Perrot negotiated a series of agreements with landholders throughout Munster to have them begin to forego the Irish system of exactions and establish freeholders along English tenurial lines. In Duhallow this manifested itself in the conclusion of agreements with several prominent O'Callaghans and O'Keeffes in May 1573 and most significantly with Owen MacDonogh, the ruling lord of Duhallow.[50] The years ahead would see further methods of political oversight and taxation introduced into Duhallow.[51] No longer could lords such as Art O'Keeffe or Donogh MacTeige O'Callaghan simply consider the English crown as a far-away, negligible threat in the manner that would have been possible in their early years as lords of Pobble O Keeffe and Pobble I Callaghan in the 1530s and 1540s.

Indeed, the advent of provincial government was leading to the emergence of concerted plans to tighten administrative control over south Munster in the mid-1570s. Duhallow was central to these. A treatise written around 1574 by Perrot argued that greater control could be achieved there by forming parts of north Kerry, west Limerick and north-west Cork including Duhallow into a new 'Queen's County'.[52] Furthermore, Perrot proposed that the lords throughout Munster should be required to extend the agreements with the commons of their lands to create freeholders across the province. In tandem, the Irish system of exactions was to be prohibited, while Perrot also proposed the cutting down of the major woods of the province whereby 'no rebel hereafter shall have any succour or place of strength in the same wood'.[53] The vast woodlands of Duhallow would be central in this project. Perrot was not the only figure putting forward schemes that would have drastic implications for Duhallow. Early in 1574 Humphrey Gilbert presented Queen Elizabeth with a 'Book' for reforming Munster, some of which was specifically designed to generate greater crown control over north-west Cork. Gilbert, for instance, recommended the establishment of a crown military garrison at Buttevant just to the north-east of Duhallow. The intention of this, Gilbert noted expressly, was to 'suppress' the MacDonoghs, O'Callaghans and O'Keeffes.[54] To aid in all this, a bridge was also proposed over the Blackwater to facilitate communications and travel between Cork and Kilmallock, Mallow lying within eyesight of the O'Callaghan lands being the obvious site for such a crossing point.[55]

Proposals of this kind were being made at a time when the political situation in Munster was becoming ever more fractious. Although the embers of FitzMaurice's rebellion had finally been quenched early in 1573 when he surrendered to the government and was pardoned, fresh unrest quickly arose. Within months FitzMaurice departed for mainland Europe to try to gather support from Catholic Spain and the papacy for an invasion of Ireland.[56] More immediately, in March 1573 Desmond had finally been allowed to depart from England to Dublin, although he was still not permitted to return to Munster. One stipulation of his release from detention from London was that he would not interfere in the affairs of the Duhallow lordships.[57] Whatever the terms of his being set at liberty from England might have been, they were not adhered to for long. Just months later, Desmond absconded without permission from the capital and returned to Munster.[58] Well over a year of unrest followed during which Desmond rallied his affinity and a new rebellion led by the earl seemed possible. Although Desmond was eventually reconciled with the Tudor government during late 1574 and 1575, the battlelines in Duhallow of any future rebellion were being drawn at the time and the government in Dublin had been informed that Melaghlin MacAuliffe was liable to join any rebellion which Desmond initiated.[59]

Details of events in Duhallow in the mid-to-late 1570s are scant, yet an indication of the continued pressure the lords there were facing to conform to governmental standards is provided by a letter-tract that Henry Sidney composed in the spring of 1576. Sidney had been reappointed as governor of Ireland in 1575 and embarked on a vice-regal progress through the entire country between the autumn of 1575 and the spring of 1576. He arrived at Cork city just before Christmas 1575 where a major conference of the lords of south Munster had been organized. To this came Art O'Keeffe and Owen MacDonogh, while Melaghlin MacAuliffe and Donogh MacTeige O'Callaghan sent their sons and supposed heirs, the two leaders claiming old age and infirmity had prevented them from attending in person.[60] They may well have disliked what they heard had they been there. Over Christmas 1575 a reform programme was promulgated at Cork whereby the lords of south Munster were to hand in lists of any soldiers in their employ and provide sureties for their good behaviour, while there was much talk of prohibiting the system of Irish exactions and replacing it with a more stable payment to the crown. Sidney surely had in mind the new 'composition' scheme through which he aimed to 'compound' with the lords of Connacht and Munster for stable taxes to be paid to the Tudor government.[61] The viceroy subsequently reported to the Privy Council in England that the lords of Munster had seemed amenable to the idea, yet how willing they would have been to acquiesce to a policy initiative explicitly designed to undermine their power base is open to question.

Sidney's conference of the Munster lords at Cork was symptomatic of the manner in which Tudor government continued to make its presence felt in the south of the country in a way that would have been unimaginable back in the 1530s. Doubtlessly this pattern of creeping oversight through forced anglicization, crown taxation and judicial oversight would have continued to increase over the years ahead under normal circumstances. But events in the years that followed dictated otherwise. In the summer of 1579 James FitzMaurice returned to Ireland with limited support from the papacy to launch a fresh rebellion in Munster. In the months that followed, Desmond was gradually drawn into the revolt, which became general throughout Munster.[62] As a consequence, from late 1579 Duhallow found itself at the geographical centre of a province-wide insurrection that sought to oust the Tudor regime from the south of Ireland. Unwittingly, the Desmond Rebellion was in the long run to accelerate the process whereby the Tudor state began to dismantle the quasi-independent lordships of the province. This would have enormous consequences for the MacDonoghs, the O'Keeffes and the O'Callaghans, and above all the MacAuliffes of Clanawley.

Overall, the years between the Kildare Rebellion in the mid-1530s and the outbreak of the Desmond Rebellion at the end of the 1570s saw a profound shift in the political landscape of Munster and Duhallow. During the first half of the sixteenth century the English state was very much a peripheral player in the affairs of Duhallow, infrequently making itself felt from far away Dublin. But as the century progressed the shadow of Dublin Castle's control was becoming ever greater. For the present time its tangible impact on Duhallow was relatively minimal, but the establishment of a provincial president and council in Munster in 1570 suggested that increasing oversight and taxation were imminent, as well as pressure to introduce the common law and establish English property norms through the creation of freeholds. More worryingly, plantation of the lands of the MacDonoghs and O'Callaghans had been given serious consideration. Equally, while no crown garrisons had yet been established within Duhallow itself, a ward of English troops had been temporarily placed at Portrinard just to the north-west of Clanawley during the FitzMaurice Rebellion, while proposals to establish bridges over the Blackwater and place permanent military outposts at sites such as Buttevant were becoming all too frequent. The years ahead would not produce any easier circumstances for the lordships of the MacDonogh-MacCarthys, O'Callaghans, MacAuliffes and O'Keeffes.

3. The crisis of lordship in late Elizabethan Duhallow, 1579–98

In June 1580 the viceroy William Pelham was at the height of his military campaigning through Munster to prosecute the earl of Desmond and his followers. On 12 June he camped with his forces near Buttevant. The following day the viceroy pushed onwards into Duhallow where he was joined by the queen's perennial servant in Ireland, the tenth earl of Ormond, Thomas Butler. Just hours later, on 14 June, Duhallow began to feel the full impact of the war that had gripped the southern province since the summer of 1579. Having made some preparations to secure the O'Callaghan lands around Clonmeen for the crown interest, Pelham marched his forces westwards through Kanturk, camping overnight by the banks of the River Owenanare running north-west from Kanturk towards the MacAuliffe strongholds of Castlemacauliffe and Carrig Castle.[1] This was enemy territory. In 1579 Melaghlin MacAuliffe, a strong adherent of Desmond's throughout the 1570s, had thrown in his lot with the earl. Although he died in December of that year, seemingly of old age, the sept was suspected of continuing adherence to Desmond's cause. Thus, after breaking camp on 15 June Pelham's forces marched '5 miles in McAuley's country, burning and defacing the same', until 'we entered the foul boggy mountain of Slievelougher'.[2] When they passed over the other side of the mountain into Kerry, a major part of the livestock of the region, collected together for safe-keeping, was captured, consisting of over two thousand cattle, as well as sheep and horses. Nor was this ravaging of Clanawley an isolated incident. Having campaigned westward towards Dingle and Castlemaine in the two weeks that followed, in late June Pelham brought his forces back east. Taking advantage of the few weeks in the year that the 'mountain of Slievelougher' was passable for a crown army, Pelham yet again campaigned through western Duhallow passing on the southern extremity of Sliabh Luachra and sending his gun-bearing troops to scan the woods for rebels as they went.[3] War had come to Duhallow.

The respective alignments of the Duhallow lords in the Desmond Rebellion were shaped early in the conflict and remained largely stationary throughout. James FitzMaurice had arrived in Kerry from continental Europe in mid-July 1579 with a small contingent of papal and Spanish troops. However, he was dead by mid-August and subsequent events pushed the earl of Desmond into a leadership position within the insurrection, which had spread across Munster, by the late autumn of 1579. In Duhallow Desmond quickly found allies from two sources.[4] In Clanawley Melaghlin MacAuliffe threw the support of the sept behind Desmond's rebellion. This was not surprising. The sept had been involved in the numerous conflicts Desmond engaged in during the 1560s and indeed in the mid-1570s Melaghlin and his close family members may well have been implicated in further unrest for which a pardon was granted in the winter of 1574.[5] The death of the elderly Melaghlin in December 1579 did not lead to any substantial shift in the allegiances of the lordship of Clanawley. His son and successor Donogh Bane continued in rebellion.[6] Additionally, owing to the seemingly perpetual conflict for control over the MacDonogh lordship, Donogh MacCormac MacDonogh, at that time *tanist* of the sept, joined the revolt in opposition to the current lord, Owen MacDonogh.[7] Following Desmond's proclamation as a rebel in early November the newly appointed viceroy Pelham sent directives to the lords of Munster commanding them to be ready to serve the crown interest in quelling the rebellion.[8] Over the four years that followed, Owen MacDonogh, Conor O'Callaghan and Art O'Keeffe remained crown loyalists, in the latter case seemingly as a stalwart ally of Dublin Castle.

The Duhallow region appears to have felt the sharpest impact of the war in its early stages during the winter of 1579/80 and the spring and summer of 1580, during which time the military effort was being prosecuted in Munster by Pelham and Ormond. The greater Sliabh Luachra region was ravaged in the winter of 1579 by Ormond, while into the spring both the viceroy and the earl continued to wage a campaign of scorched earth in Desmond's strongholds throughout south Limerick, north Cork and north Kerry.[9] This campaign extended into the heart of Duhallow itself in the summer of 1580.

Pelham's campaign at this time was justified by him on the failure of the Duhallow lords to appear at a viceregal audience at Limerick in May.[10] The result was the devastation of the MacAuliffe lands, while even those of ostensible loyalists such as Conor O'Callaghan were impacted on by the crown armies. As elsewhere in Munster, this brutal approach did produce results in Duhallow. In the later summer Donogh MacAuliffe and Donogh MacCormac MacDonogh sought terms and were temporarily pardoned.[11] This was in keeping with Desmond's generally waning position in the second half of 1580 and for a time it appeared as though peace terms would be negotiated. However, the appointment of the broadly incompetent Arthur, Lord Grey de Wilton, as Pelham's successor in the vice-regal office, along with the simultaneous outbreak of a further rebellion in the Pale led by the Viscount Baltinglass, buoyed Desmond's fortunes.[12] The rebellion would persist for several years.

Owing to Duhallow's geographical position at the centre of military operations, plans began to abound at the height of the war to improve crown control over north-west Cork. In a 'Discourse' he composed in 1580, Pelham proposed erecting a bridge over the Blackwater at Mallow, specifically noting that the river rose in the Sliabh Luachra region of western Duhallow and that a bridging point would improve communications between Cork and Kilmallock. Resurrecting an abortive initiative of the FitzMaurice Rebellion ten years earlier, Pelham also recommend the garrisoning of Portrinard near Abbeyfeale.[13] Two years later the prominent army captain Edward Barkley suggested placing large garrisons at Mallow and Kilmallock on the near outskirts of Duhallow. Barkley envisaged that no fewer than one hundred horse and five hundred kern should be stationed at Mallow, with twenty-five horse and two hundred foot at Kilmallock, forces which would have had serious implications for the autonomy of the Duhallow lordships if they were to have been positioned at these sites.[14] Others such as Ormond continued to argue for a bridge and settlement at Mallow right down to the close of the rebellion, foreshadowing developments during the post-war reconstruction.[15]

The course of the war shifted in 1582 as Grey's revocation and the restoration of Ormond as head of the war effort saw Desmond's fortunes ebb. One of his last successes was enjoyed in September

1582 when along with several allies including Donogh MacCormac MacDonogh he invaded Pobble O Keeffe. Art O'Keeffe subsequently followed the earl's forces back west into Sliabh Luachra where a battle resulted in the deaths of eighty of O'Keeffe's followers, as well as the capture of the lord himself and several of his followers including his son Art Óge. Another son, Hugh, was killed during the confrontation, perhaps ensuring that when the elderly Art died in 1583, shortly after his release, Art Óge succeeded him.[16] This transient victory for Desmond in the autumn of 1582 aside, his position in Munster continued to deteriorate. The crown's offer of general pardons to those who had partaken in the rebellion stripped the earl of supporters through late 1582.[17] By 1583 he was reduced to a small group of followers moving between successive hiding places. Much of their time was spent in the mountainous, inaccessible region of Sliabh Luachra in west Duhallow and north Kerry.[18] Thus, even though Donogh MacCormac MacDonogh, one of Desmond's most stalwart allies, submitted to the crown in April 1583, Donogh MacAuliffe continued to shelter Desmond in the wilderness of western Clanawley as late as October 1583.[19] It soon ended. On 11 November Desmond and his last few adherents were surrounded and slaughtered in the Glanageenty Woods on the western outskirts of Sliabh Luachra in north Kerry.[20]

The rebellion was over. The impact, however, had been immense. Writing many years later, Edmund Spenser famously described the devastation, starvation and loss of life he witnessed in Munster at the height of the war. More immediately, Warham St Leger suggested that by the spring of 1582 at least thirty thousand people had died throughout the province owing to war and famine.[21] Duhallow had not escaped this desolation. The same writer in October 1582 noted that the region was completely waste, as were the adjoining countries of the Roches and Barrys eastwards towards Fermoy.[22] There is no way of estimating with any certitude the demographic and economic consequences for the Duhallow region, but they must have been considerable given the centrality of north-west Cork to the war's theatre of operations.

The political implications are more measurable. While the MacDonoghs, O'Keeffes and O'Callaghans and minor septs such as the MacQuirkes and the Magners were generally excused for any minor infractions committed during the conflict, the MacAuliffes were to face severe punishment. Donogh MacAuliffe had died in a conflict with his nephew Teige in 1583.[23] He was succeeded by his brother, Melaghlin MacMelaghlin MacAuliffe, but this new lord inherited a precarious position.[24] As the sept were deemed to have been in rebellion throughout the war and the elderly Melaghlin had died in rebellion in December 1579 the MacAuliffe lands were now judged by the crown to be attainted and confiscated to the crown.[25] Consequently, while Melaghlin MacMelaghlin was still effectively in control of Clanawley in 1583 his position was no longer recognized by the crown. There is no evidence to indicate how the authorities in Dublin viewed the case in the years that followed, but it would appear that there was some indecision as to whether the MacAuliffe lands would be included in the official plantation of Desmond and his allies' lands throughout Munster which was initiated following the war. This would certainly explain why the government waited until June 1587 before it bestowed the bulk of the Clanawley lands on one Patrick Graunt of Waterford.[26] This eventual resolution might have only been reached following renewed unrest of some kind among the leading MacAuliffes in the spring of 1587.[27] Consequently, the major political fallout from the Desmond Rebellion was that the MacAuliffe lordship now ceased to be legitimate from the crown's perspective. Rather it was now confiscated under the common law. The implications of this in practice in 1583 must have been minimal and, without a garrison in the region to enforce the crown's will, the MacAuliffes would have simply gone back to farming their lands and overseeing their tenants. Over time though, the dispensation of 1583 would have an immense bearing on western and northern Duhallow.

In the aftermath of the Desmond Rebellion the situation in the MacDonogh lordship returned to what it had been in the pre-war period. The rivalry between the two senior branches of the sept, the family lines of Cormac and Owen MacDonogh, continued unremittingly in the post-1583 period, and indeed intensified. The ruling lord at the outset of the rebellion was Owen MacDermot MacDonogh. His loyalties during the war are hard to precisely identify. Generally, Owen seems to have been a crown loyalist, though one of questionable fidelity, and he was detained at some point between 1580 and 1582 at Limerick. Less ambiguous was the

bearing of Donogh MacCormac MacDonogh, Owen's *tanist* and a
rival for power from the MacCormac branch of the sept. Donogh
was a faithful adherent of Desmond's for most of the rebellion. In
1582 he found himself confronted by a shifting situation in Duhallow
as Owen MacDermot died in Limerick at this time, leaving the
MacOwen branch of the sept headed by Owen's son Dermot, a young
man perhaps little more than a teenager in 1582.[28] Given Donogh
MacCormac's robust support for Desmond throughout the rebellion
one would assume that the crown would have been unequivocal in its
support for Dermot MacOwen to hold the rule of the MacDonogh
lordship in the aftermath of his father's death. And yet the regime
equivocated. In the early winter of 1584 Donogh was granted a
full pardon and in the years ahead would emerge as the preferred
candidate to rule the lordship.[29] Dermot, however, was not to be
outdone. When a new parliament was held at Dublin in 1585 the two
rivals both attended, doubtlessly the better to present their individual
claims to the lordship.[30] So began a bitter struggle for control of the
MacDonogh lordship, one which would continue between Donogh
and Dermot for the better part of two decades.

  Such instability at the heart of Duhallow occurred as momentous
change was underway throughout Munster. In the aftermath of
the Desmond Rebellion the crown elected to undertake a closely
monitored state-run plantation of more than 300,000 statute acres
across Munster, the core of this being Desmond's former lands in
Limerick, north Kerry, various parts of Cork and west Waterford.
Surveying and planning were initiated in 1584 and continued through
the mid-1580s. By 1586 the scheme was effectively finalized. Estates
of 4,000, 8,000 and 12,000 acres were to be granted to individual
undertakers who would undertake to settle these lands with English
tenants and erect English settlements thereon. In time it was envisaged
that these would lead to the fostering of a new English society
throughout Munster replete with towns, markets and law courts.[31]
The plantation did not directly impact on Duhallow. As noted, the
MacDonoghs, O'Callaghans and O'Keeffes were not sufficiently
implicated in Desmond's rebellion to justify crown expropriation of
their lands. Full pardons were accordingly granted to figures such as
Conor O'Callaghan and Art Óge O'Keeffe in the summer of 1585.[32]
The MacAuliffe lands could have been included, but for unclear

reasons were omitted from the official plantation scheme and instead granted privately to Patrick Graunt in 1587. Perhaps geography played a part also in this decision. After all, the plantation commissioners in 1587 deliberated over whether the undertakers who received lands in the Sliabh Luachra vicinity in west Limerick and north Kerry ought to be excused having to settle quite so many English planters on their new estates, the region being so mountainous and impenetrable that it would be harder to draw settlers to live there.[33]

Whatever the motives for the omission of Clanawley from the official plantation scheme, Duhallow was still substantially affected by the initiative. It was now surrounded by plantation estates. To the north of Duhallow, just over the Limerick border, Sir William Courtenay received the Newcastle seignory just a few kilometres from the northern outskirts of Clanawley. Courtenay's grant was particularly noteworthy for including the fort of Portrinard near Abbeyfeale, the stronghold that had been garrisoned at the height of the FitzMaurice Rebellion.[34] To the west planters such as Sir William Herbert, Sir Edward Denny and Sir Valentine Browne were given estates running from Tralee, Castlemaine and Castleisland in north Kerry further inland to the western outskirts of Duhallow. The presence of these newcomers on the periphery of the lands of the MacAuliffes and O'Keeffes would have been tangible. Denny's grant of his estate included a provision that he could freely avail of pasturage for his livestock on the mountain of Sliabh Luachra, while Herbert's grant contained a stipulation that he would also be given the manor house of Brosna lying a few kilometres from the MacAuliffe and O'Keeffe lordships.[35] Finally, to the east numerous estates now bordered or closely bordered Duhallow. Hugh Cuffe had, for instance, been granted the Kilmore seignory directly to the north-east. Most critical, however, was the Mallow seignory, which was bestowed at the outset of the plantation to Sir Thomas Norris. Norris was a brother of the recently appointed lord president of Munster, Sir John Norris. John would serve as president throughout most of the 1580s and 1590s, but his role was nominal, he often being absent on military campaigns elsewhere in Europe. Accordingly, Thomas served as the de-facto president from the early 1580s through to the late 1590s. Governing the province from his new base at Mallow as vice-president of Munster, he posed an unprecedented challenge to the independence of the lords of Duhallow.[36] The O'Callaghan lordship, in particular, was now closely watched over by the senior crown officer in Munster, whose estate at Mallow was just downriver from the O'Callaghan strongholds at Dromaneen and Clonmeen. Consequently, the last fifteen or so years of the reign of Elizabeth I saw the emergence of a much greater depth of knowledge within government of the political arrangements prevailing in east Duhallow.[37] Therefore, while the Munster Plantation did not directly impact on Duhallow, it nevertheless dramatically altered the political situation in north-west Cork.

As the Munster Plantation was being initiated in the late 1580s the rivalry between Donogh MacCormac and Dermot MacOwen for control over the MacDonogh lordship was intensifying. In 1588 Ireland entered a major crisis as the remains of the Spanish Armada crashed ashore along the coast of the second Tudor kingdom. The newly appointed viceroy, William FitzWilliam, was charged with arresting or slaughtering the several thousand Spanish troops which had made landfall in Ulster, Connacht and Munster. In this emergency the government moved to temporarily arrest many individuals of doubtful loyalty. Among these in Munster were Donogh MacCormac and the White Knight, Edmund FitzGibbon.[38] Over the next several months a debate emerged within government circles as to what should be done with the claimant to the lordship of Duhallow. Thomas Norris was relatively mild in his recommendations, suggesting that the MacDonogh lordship should be divided between Donogh and Dermot, the better to dilute both individuals' power.[39] However, writing that winter to the lord treasurer of England, William Cecil, Lord Burghley, Warham St Leger argued that former rebels such as Donogh should be executed to prevent any unrest.[40] The more moderate course ultimately won the day. Donogh was released from imprisonment in January 1589 once the Armada emergency had passed.[41] Within weeks, though, Dermot MacOwen was granted livery of his lands that had been withheld since his father's death in 1582.[42] As a consequence the two rivals were now set on a collision course that would roll on into the 1590s. In the early summer of 1590 Donogh arrived in London with the White Knight, whose daughter Donogh had recently married and whose lands lay to the north and east of Fermoy.[43] Presenting a unified front, the pair pressed

Donogh's claim to the headship of the MacDonogh lordship. It met with success, perhaps largely owing to Donogh's offer to hold the lordship in the crown's name if acknowledged by the queen.[44] When he returned to Ireland the former rebel, who had only recently been imprisoned during the Armada crisis, was effectively the crown's preferred candidate to the title of lord of Duhallow.[45] Dermot MacOwen's response to his being superseded by Donogh was swift. In the spring of 1591 he made his own way to England to present his countersuit at court.[46] This was heard in May, however Dermot was left waiting on a decision until September.[47] When it came it was positive and represented a complete *volte-face* by the metropolitan government, which now decided to back Dermot's claim and in December he returned to Ireland with letters to that effect.[48] In these the Privy Council laid out their understanding of the competing claims to the lordship going back to the days of Henry VIII, and their assertion that they had been misled by Donogh when he had visited court in the summer of 1590.[49] And yet things did not resolve themselves even then. The uncertainty within government continued and Donogh pressed a further counterclaim that autumn.[50] As a result the perennial rivalry endured into the mid-1590s and would have substantial implications when rebellion yet again engulfed the southern province in the autumn of 1598.

The vacillating behaviour of the crown in switching its support between Donogh and Dermot throughout the late 1580s and early 1590s was undertaken purely in the interest of arriving at the most advantageous dispensation for the Tudor state. The crown was shifting its position to find the most beneficial candidate to install at Kanturk and its environs. Central to this were the respective offers being made to hold the lordship of the queen. Such offers, whereby an Irish lord would acknowledge the crown as the suzerain power of Ireland and make some limited professions of their intention to anglicize their lordships in return for crown support for their position, were becoming common in Ireland by the 1580s. These were effectively a watered-down version of the 'surrender and regrant' arrangements undertaken in the 1540s, but without offers of English nobility. In the summer of 1588 and again in the summer of 1590 Donogh MacCormac explicitly offered to hold the MacDonogh lordship in the name of the crown if his suit was favoured over Dermot's.[51] Equally,

Dermot was asserting his own willingness to do so when he travelled to court in person for six months of 1591 to press his claims. Indeed, such offers went back further. In the late 1570s before the outbreak of the Desmond Rebellion Owen MacDonogh, Dermot's father, had petitioned to surrender his land and to have a regrant of the lordship of Duhallow and the manor of Kanturk from the crown. The Privy Council in England had at that time commanded the administration in Dublin to investigate what other Irish lords of the region might be amenable to such an arrangement.[52] While the war temporarily interrupted such plans, they were revived thereafter.

In one prominent instance within Duhallow a major agreement of this kind was even concluded. In late 1592 or early 1593 a petition was presented to the government on behalf of several Irish lords of Co. Cork, one being Conor O'Callaghan. Conor, in imitation of his neighbours among the MacDonoghs, had determined that crown recognition of his position was the best means of securing it into the future. Accordingly, O'Callaghan offered to surrender his lands in return for a regrant and a commitment to anglicize the law and systems of landholding in Pobble I Callaghan.[53] Curiously, or perhaps typically, the government did not act speedily on this offer. FitzWilliam was ordered by the regime in London to investigate the feasibility of the offer in the spring of 1593, but it took until the summer of 1594 for the viceroy to order Thomas Norris to inquire into the extent and value of O'Callaghan's lands as a preparatory to a surrender.[54] The result was an extensive inquisition taken at Mallow on 25 October 1594 before Norris and the leading legal officers of Munster and at which the full extent of the O'Callaghan lands were determined.[55] This achieved, a few weeks later, on 2 December 1594, the crown formally accepted the surrender by Conor O'Callaghan of his lands of Dromaneen and Clonmeen. Five days later these lands were regranted by the crown, to hold them henceforward under English tenure by knight's service, paying a crown rent and promising to forego the system of Irish feudal dues.[56] Here, finally, in late 1594 was the most striking movement yet towards one of the Irish lords of Duhallow being transformed into an English-style noble.

This was not an isolated development. Efforts to introduce English methods of taxation into the Irish polity and curb recourse to the Irish system of exactions had been a cornerstone of Tudor government in

Ireland throughout the sixteenth century. One such approach had emerged in the early 1570s. Known to posterity as 'composition', the policy involved the Irish lords 'compounding' to begin taking fixed taxes from their tenants in lieu of the Irish exactions such as 'coign and livery'. The resulting 'composition' tax paid by newly established English-style freeholders would then allow the lord to pay taxes to the crown. This novel tax would supersede previous forms of crown taxation and, it was envisaged, would make the Dublin government self-sustaining. 'Composition' had been championed by Sidney upon his reappointment in 1575. In the years that followed concerted efforts were made to implement it in a concerted fashion in Connacht, and more sporadically in parts of Munster and Leinster.[57] Now, in the early 1590s FitzWilliam's government set about imposing 'composition' on those Irish lords in county Cork whose lands had not been included in the plantation.[58] On 17 September 1592 an arrangement was reached with the lords of Duhallow whereby a composition taxation of £30 sterling per annum would be paid to the crown. This would be divided into three portions, with the O'Callaghans paying £10, the MacDonoghs paying the second £10, and the final £10 being taxed collectively on Clanawley, the O'Keeffes and the MacQuirkes. The agreement was signed by Conor O'Callaghan and Art Óge O'Keeffe, while Dermot MacOwen had sent a letter to O'Keeffe to signify his agreement thereto.[59] As such, here in 1592 the Duhallow lords were enjoined to enter a formal system of crown taxation in Munster. It would, however, quickly be overtaken by events. A proviso within the agreement stipulated that this 'composition' would be superseded by other contributions and extraordinary taxes if a military emergency developed. This would come sooner than any of the signatories might have expected in September 1592.

One final substantial development occurred within Duhallow prior to the outbreak of that conflict. Although the MacAuliffes were attainted for their involvement in Desmond's rebellion and their lands were eventually given to Patrick Graunt in 1587, the lordship had not been more substantially dismantled in the aftermath of the conflict. Indeed, in the summer of 1585 the new head of the sept, Melaghlin MacMelaghlin MacAuliffe, was one of many individuals in the county to receive a pardon for his participation in the uprising.[60] The exact dynamics of how Clanawley was governed in the years that followed from Graunt's receipt of the MacAuliffe lands in 1587 are unclear, but it seems probable that his ownership changed things little on the ground in north-west Duhallow. This would certainly explain developments in 1592. Early that year Melaghlin MacAuliffe travelled in person to court in England. His mission was clear. Melaghlin appealed to Elizabeth's government that his father could not possibly have been as active a participant in Desmond's rebellion as had been supposed as he was blind and bed-ridden in 1579. Consequently, the confiscation of the MacAuliffe lands and their bestowal on Graunt should be reversed.[61] This mission proved substantially successful. In November 1592, shortly after his return to Ireland, MacAuliffe had Graunt's deed of 1587 passed to him.[62] Thus, almost a decade after the end of the Desmond Rebellion, the MacAuliffes found themselves partially restored to a position of legitimacy in the eyes of the crown in north-west Duhallow.

The mid-to-late 1590s could have seen a continuing drift towards the anglicization of Duhallow. However, events elsewhere were to deem otherwise. Recent studies of the Nine Years War have argued convincingly that its origins should be traced to a localized rebellion within the Maguire lordship in Fermanagh in 1593. The second earl of Tyrone, Hugh O'Neill, maintained a façade of loyalty to the crown at this time, but Maguire's revolt was effectively a proxy war by Tyrone. When he moved into outright rebellion himself a year later it was unsurprising to many senior English officials in Ireland. The war was ostensibly caused by developments in Ulster which substantially mirrored those in Munster. The imposition of English county government, including the holding of regional courts, the introduction of crown taxation and the placing of garrisons across Ulster, were all major factors in the drift towards confrontation in the north. Especially incendiary were efforts to divide power within the northern lordships such as those of the MacMahons, O'Reillys and Maguires between competing branches of the ruling septs, while the appointment of several provocative sheriffs in Donegal and elsewhere made the situation highly combustible by 1593. When war finally came it would be characterized in its early years by a mixture of a stop-start phoney war and sporadic peace negotiations, with the Ulster confederates simultaneously seeking military and financial aid from Philip II of Spain.[63]

At this stage the theatre of military operations was spread across Ulster, with forays by O'Donnell into Connacht, O'Neill south into the Pale, and large pockets of insurrection caused by Tyrone's allies in Leinster. Munster, however, was virtually untouched by the rebellion. Nevertheless, the provincial government in the south remained on alert throughout the mid-1590s. In 1594 Florence MacCarthy Reagh, a relative of the deceased earl of Desmond and direct heir of the MacCarthy Reagh branch of the Munster MacCarthys, having only recently been released from imprisonment in London, reported from Ireland that Dermot MacOwen MacDonogh was greatly discontented with the crown's handling of the dispute within the Duhallow lordship over the past years and was likely to enter rebellion if the war spread to Munster.[64] An anonymous policy paper composed around 1596 also recommended that some of the Munster septs such as the O'Callaghans needed to be handled carefully given the volatile situation elsewhere in Ireland.[65] There was then a definite awareness in these early stages of the Nine Years War that the southern province could experience a considerable insurrection if the circumstances became propitious to do so. In the end when the rebellion did reach the south it exploded like a powder-keg and demolished the embryonic plantation. Those events will be explored in the following chapter.

The second half of the reign of Elizabeth I witnessed very great changes in Duhallow. Gone were the days of the 1560s when figures like Melaghlin MacAuliffe, Art O'Keeffe and Donogh MacTeige O'Callaghan were almost entirely independent of Dublin Castle. The crown's position had been strengthened by the establishment of a provincial government in Munster in 1570. But it was the Desmond Rebellion with its unprecedented level of military confrontation between the Tudor state and the lords of Munster that truly transformed the political landscape of the southern province and threw the lordships of Duhallow into crisis. Mass plantation across much of the province followed in the wake of the war. Duhallow managed to avoid being involved in this, with only the MacAuliffes suffering the confiscation of their lands in the post-1583 settlement. Nevertheless, the impact of the plantation was considerable. To the west of Clanawley and Pobble O Keeffe in east and north Kerry planters such as William Herbert and Edward Denny now had grazing rights on Sliabh Luachra. Most jarringly, the O'Callaghans had to contend with the de-facto lord president of Munster, Thomas Norris, having established his provincial government at Mallow within eyesight of their lordship. It is unsurprising considering all these circumstances that the early 1590s saw the Duhallow lords offering to hold their lands of Queen Elizabeth and entering into 'composition' taxation arrangements. Yet, while all of this was indicative of great change and increasing political crisis within the Duhallow lordships, it was not to go unopposed. When, in 1598, Tyrone and his allies began to look like they could ultimately prove victorious in their confrontation with the crown, the lords of Duhallow elected to join the revolt in Munster in the hope that the growing power of the Tudor state in southern Ireland could be pushed back.

4. Duhallow and the Nine Years War, 1598–1603

On 29 September 1598 Owny O'More, the last major head of the O'Mores of Laois, and Richard Tyrrell, a scion of the Gaelicized Old English Tyrrells of Westmeath, two of the foremost rebel leaders in Leinster, led a contingent of troops south-west from the midlands into Tipperary. The Leinster rebels were buoyant in the late autumn of 1598. Weeks earlier, on 14 August, a crown army of nearly four thousand troops had been badly defeated by O'Neill and his forces as they attempted to resupply the crown garrison at the Blackwater fort in southern Ulster. The Battle of the Yellow Ford, as it has become known, was the greatest defeat of English arms in Ireland during the sixteenth century, with approximately 1,500 men killed in the space of a few hours.[1] In the weeks after it, the war spread rapidly throughout Ireland as the crown's military position became critical. O'More and Tyrrell's mission in late September was to extend the insurrection into Munster. In the weeks that followed the rebellion spread like wildfire across the south. The rebels swept south-west towards Limerick and Cork as many Irish lords who were disaffected with the post-Desmond Rebellion dispensation threw in their lot with Tyrone and his allies. One of them was James FitzThomas FitzGerald, a bastard grandson of the fourteenth earl of Desmond who had died in 1558. Within days of the extension of the rebellion south into Munster FitzGerald had laid claim to the dormant earldom of Desmond.[2] Others followed suit, reasserting claims to Irish titles which had effectively been prohibited by the Elizabethan regime. As the military insurrection spread, violence increased. The hyperbolic nature of some of the English reportage of these events makes it difficult to determine the precise scale of atrocities on English civilians, but undoubtedly scores if not hundreds of English plantation settlers were killed throughout the south in October. A mass exodus of the colonists towards the walled towns ensued from where many took ship for England. By the end of October 1598 the plantation had effectively been destroyed and Munster became a major front in the Nine Years War.[3]

The immediate impact of these events on Duhallow is not entirely clear. Indeed it is not even wholly clear where the loyalties of the respective lords of Clanawley, Pobble O Keeffe, Pobble I Callaghan, and the smaller polities such as the MacQuirkes and the O'Mullanes lay in 1598, though the situation regarding the MacDonoghs is certainly less ambiguous. Clearly though the region was ripe for rebellion.[4] A later inquisition of 1604 even suggests that Donogh MacCormac had entered into rebellion early on in the outbreak of troubles in Ulster around 1595.[5] Writing towards the end of October 1598 when Munster had been overrun, Arthur Hyde, who had received a significant plantation estate near Fermoy, noted that the rebels throughout Munster had risen as soon as O'More and Tyrrell had led their troops into the province in the closing days of September and that first among them to join the war were Dermot MacOwen MacDonogh and his nemesis Donogh MacCormac. A temporary rapprochement had occurred between the two rival MacDonoghs and a compromise was reached. Donogh was now to be unhindered in his long-running claim to the lordship of Duhallow, while in a novel twist Dermot was styling himself as a new earl of Clancar and MacCarthy Mór, the previous first earl having died in 1596.[6] Consequently, the pair combined to attack Hyde's residence at Carrigeneady near Fermoy in mid-October.[7] Given the prominence of the two chief MacDonoghs in the rebellion it is little surprise to find Ormond reporting that Mallow was on the brink of collapse to a rebel onslaught within less than three weeks of the beginning of the insurrection.[8] There is little direct information in the records of the time of the actions of Conor O'Callaghan, Art Óge O'Keeffe or Melaghlin MacAuliffe, yet they were clearly active participants in the rebellion. A governmental memorandum of the spring of 1599 lists them as such and towards late October 1598 Norris reported to London that almost all the Irish had joined the rebellion.[9]

The crown's response to these developments fluctuated with the changing conditions in the months ahead, but a strategy to confront the more specific situation in Duhallow was worked out swiftly. Since Donogh MacCormac and Dermot MacOwen had been rivals for the better part of twenty years, that rivalry should be exploited.

In November 1598 the English secretary of state, Sir Robert Cecil, wrote to Norris commanding him to try to negotiate with Donogh, who had limited his ambitions to claiming the lordship of Duhallow, over Dermot, whose much more ambitious designs on the title of MacCarthy Mór had made him the greater threat in the eyes of the metropolitan government. Accordingly, Norris should persuade Donogh that he would be installed as head of the MacDonogh lordship if he was willing to ally with the crown and bend his resources against Dermot.[10] Donogh, however, was not to be dissuaded from his defiance so easily. It took until the early spring of 1599 for this directive to reach Norris. When it did he responded that Donogh and many others in Munster had already made overtures for peace negotiations but that these were half-hearted, the Irish lords being fully aware of how weak the crown's position was early in 1599.[11] The appointment of a new viceroy to oversee the suppression of the rebellion throughout the country did not help matters. When Robert Devereux, second earl of Essex, arrived in Ireland in April 1599 he was given charge of a crown army which, at over seventeen thousand men, eclipsed the size of any seen in Ireland under the Tudors. With such forces at his disposal it augured ill for the Munster rebels that Essex's first action was to campaign south in the summer of 1599. But Devereux's operation proved largely ineffective and, other than shoring up the crown's position in Tipperary through the capture of Cahir Castle, achieved nothing of consequence.[12] Moreover, the death of Norris in August 1599, having suffered a serious injury in a skirmish near Limerick during the summer, deprived the crown of its chief commander in Munster.[13]

Evidently a new strategy was needed. The best available was that which had been used to crush numerous regional wars in Ireland throughout Elizabeth's reign: a garrison strategy. In early October 1599 the chief justice of Munster, William Saxey, seemingly unaware that Essex had returned to England without permission following a parley with O'Neill in late September, wrote to the earl outlining such a stratagem. The province, Saxey argued, might best be reduced by establishing a network of large garrisons at Bantry, Mallow, Fermoy, Limerick, Kilmallock and Askeaton. These were to be considerable. For instance, three hundred infantry and twenty-five cavalry were to be stationed at Mallow, with a similar size force at the other sites.[14]

The implications for Duhallow were clear, and the appointment of such forces to Mallow and Kilmallock would have acted as a major threat to the MacDonogh rivals and the others in rebellion within the barony. Although Essex's tenure as Irish viceroy had come to an abrupt end, Saxey resubmitted the letter-tract to Cecil a few weeks later.[15] What the influence of this paper was is unclear, but a garrison strategy in Munster such as the chief justice had proposed came into operation in the months ahead.

As elsewhere in Ireland the course of the Nine Years War in Munster shifted considerably in 1600. On 23 February 1600 George Carew, an experienced military commander who had served periodically in Ireland since the mid-1570s, landed at Howth on a ship on which Charles Blount, eighth baron Mountjoy, was also a passenger.[16] Following Essex's disastrous viceroyalty and Norris's death, Mountjoy had been appointed as lord deputy of Ireland with Carew enjoined to take up the position of lord president of Munster. Over the next three years Mountjoy would oversee the crown's war effort in Ulster and Leinster, with Carew tackling matters in the south. The new lord president quickly proceeded to Munster where he compiled an extensive report to the Privy Council on how he found affairs there. There were, Carew and his council reported, as many as seven thousand rebels ranging throughout Munster and the unrest was great. The biggest threat, Carew asserted, was Florence MacCarthy Reagh. The son and heir of the deceased Sir Donough MacCarthy Reagh, the head of the second most senior branch of the Munster MacCarthys, Florence was also a relative of the FitzGeralds of Desmond and had a strong claim to be the head of the MacCarthys throughout Munster. He had been imprisoned in London during the early 1590s but had returned to Ireland on the eve of the Nine Years War in 1593. Now Carew suggested Florence had become a fulcrum for disaffection in Munster and that many of the rebels were coalescing around him. To the fore of these were Melaghlin MacAuliffe, Art Óge O'Keeffe and many of the O'Callaghans.[17] The situation was somewhat different with Conor O'Callaghan and Carew was soon writing to Cecil to describe the lord of Pobble I Callaghan as being among the 'best sort' in Munster. In mid-June Conor and many of his followers were among the first of those implicated in the rebellion in Munster to receive crown pardons.[18]

Throughout this period the situation with the two principal heads of the MacDonoghs remained fluid. An uneasy alliance had existed between Donogh MacCormac and Dermot MacOwen since the autumn of 1598, however Dermot had clearly been favoured more by Tyrone. It was perhaps unsurprising then that in late 1599 Donogh was gravitating towards Florence MacCarthy, who was himself inclined towards an alliance with the crown. Whatever the exact machinations we find Donogh being placed under arrest by Tyrone in late 1599.[19] The would-be lord of Duhallow was taken to Ulster where he remained a prisoner through 1600.[20] But his detention was to be cut short towards the end of the year as events in Munster in the summer and autumn changed Tyrone's stance towards Dermot. In the early autumn of 1600 complaints reached O'Neill of Dermot's heavy-handed behaviour in respect of his neighbours in central Munster.[21] More worryingly, information would have arrived in Ulster weeks later that Dermot and Melaghlin MacAuliffe had made an offer to the crown to surrender on terms in early August.[22] This was accepted shortly afterwards and Dermot was belatedly granted a pardon the following spring.[23] Thus, at some stage in the early winter of 1600 Donogh was released from his imprisonment in the north. He returned to Munster, but his homecoming was nevertheless short-lived. In March 1601 he appears to have been mortally wounded in a skirmish in the territory of the O'Shaughnessys in Carbery, south of Duhallow near Bandon.[24] Meanwhile, the government's pressure on Duhallow continued. In November 1600 Francis Barkley campaigned south from Limerick into Clanawley where, despite the crown's recent truce with Dermot MacOwen and Melaghlin MacAuliffe, he ravaged the MacAuliffe lands, killing numerous individuals and seizing over one thousand cattle.[25] On the surface this might appear like a highly inflammatory act, but of all the Duhallow lords Melaghlin's recent peace agreement with the crown seemed but lukewarm, and the bulk of the other senior members of the sept, including Melaghlin's own sons, John and Dermot, remained in rebellion.[26]

Ultimately, these localized developments in north-west Cork were of only moderate strategic significance to the overall course of the Nine Years War. The critical developments were happening elsewhere, primarily in Ulster. While Carew had been handling the war effort in the south, Mountjoy had tackled O'Neill and his

confederates in the north. A three-pronged front was opened, with
Captain Henry Docwra leading a naval expedition to Derry on
the north coast, Captain Arthur Chichester undertaking military
proceedings in east Ulster, and Mountjoy attempting to strike
at Tyrone from southern Ulster. Employing a series of garrisons
and rampaging armies that devastated the countryside, by 1601
Mountjoy's campaign of attrition was beginning to sow starvation
throughout Ulster and slowly wear down O'Neill and his allies. It
was at this critical juncture that foreign aid began to materialize.
Since the outbreak of the war O'Neill and O'Donnell had been
seeking aid from Spain in their revolt. Yet, despite regular promises
of support and periodic injections of financial and logistical aid, no
military expedition from Spain was forthcoming. Now, in 1601, this
finally materialized. Phillip III dispatched an armada for Ireland of
some thirty-three ships carrying 4,500 troops under the command of
Don Juan del Águila in August 1601. Poor weather scattered the fleet
on its way so that when a decision was taken to make landfall on the
coast of Munster near Kinsale del Águila's forces were much reduced.
Nevertheless, the Spanish commander quickly seized Kinsale. In
the weeks that followed it would become the crucible of the war in
Ireland as Mountjoy, Carew, Tyrone, O'Donnell and all others raced
to gather their forces and make for the southern town.[27]

Duhallow's role in these events is largely hidden from view. As
rumours of the armada abounded in the late summer Carew had
Dermot MacOwen arrested, promising the lord that he would release
him if the reports of an invasion proved unfounded, or once the
emergency had passed.[28] Dermot remained under arrest well into 1602
and, with Donogh MacCormac dead, the role of the MacDonoghs in
aiding Tyrone and his confederates at Kinsale was uncoordinated.[29]
There is virtually no mention of the O'Callaghans among the extant
records at this time, but it seems that Conor *na Cairrce* remained
loyal to the crown throughout the Kinsale emergency. The situation
was different with the O'Keeffes and the MacAuliffes. Pardons and
surrender agreements involving Art Óge O'Keeffe and his sons, Manus
and Art, in 1602 in the aftermath of Kinsale suggest that the head of
Pobble O Keeffe and his family did involve themselves to some extent
with Tyrone and O'Donnell at Kinsale.[30] The MacAuliffes' position
was less ambiguous and Melaghlin MacAuliffe and his sons, John and

Dermot, clearly fought on the confederates' side. Some intrigue may have ensued in the early winter as Hugh O'Donnell passed through Clanawley and Pobble O Keeffe on his way towards Kinsale, during which journey *The Annals of the Four Masters* later claimed he gathered allies from among the lords of every country he passed through.[31]

The finale to the Spanish intervention in Ireland would occur over the early winter and Christmas of 1601. O'Neill and O'Donnell had advanced to just north of Kinsale by the first week of December with some 5,500 infantry and nearly one thousand cavalry. With their contingents the northern lords encircled Mountjoy's forces which were already besieging the Spanish in the town. Hence, the Spanish found themselves besieged by Mountjoy's army, while the lord deputy was in turn besieged by Tyrone, O'Donnell and their allies. As disease and starvation set in for the Spanish and the crown forces, the situation looked increasingly desperate for both. At this juncture del Águila urged Tyrone to attack the English position, a decision that was to prove fatal. A dual assault was planned for the night of 24 December 1601 but, owing to poor communications, the Spanish did not get the signal to advance out of Kinsale. In the battle that ensued between O'Neill's and Mountjoy's forces, the Irish were heavily defeated, their lines having broken quite early in the battle as Christmas morning dawned. Exact numbers of casualties on both sides are unclear but O'Neill and O'Donnell appear to have lost well over a thousand men in contrast to perhaps a few dozen on the English side. In the hours that followed, the northern lords' forces dispersed from Kinsale in complete disarray.

In the aftermath of Kinsale the focus of the conflict switched back to Ulster where a war of attrition was initiated. It took until the spring of 1603 for O'Neill, his forces decimated and Ulster devastated by famine, to surrender to Mountjoy. In Munster Carew commenced with mopping up operations in the spring of 1602. Art Óge O'Keeffe and his son and future heir Manus were, for instance, included among an enormous list of individuals pardoned throughout Munster in February 1602.[32] Dermot MacOwen was most likely released at some stage in the second half of 1602. Melaghlin MacAuliffe appears to have been imprisoned at this time and remained under detention for well over a year.[33] In the summer of 1602 Carew began the final effort to crush the last remnants of the rebellion in west Cork, including

Duhallow, when he removed the country's livestock there into east
Cork and major garrisons were established at Mallow, Askeaton
and Kilmallock.[34] The aftermath of Kinsale also saw the flight of
a substantial number of prominent Duhallow individuals from
Ireland, primarily to Spain. Numerous MacAuliffes as well as a few
O'Callaghans and O'Keeffes are listed as being in Spanish service
in the years ahead. As such, defeat in the Nine Years War and the
general crisis of the Irish lordships of north-west Cork during the late
Elizabethan period led to the first substantial movement of Duhallow
émigrés leaving Ireland for the Continent in the early modern
period.[35]

Duhallow had been devastated by half a decade of conflict.[36] In
the summer of 1602 Carew reported that the entirety of western
and northern Cork was utterly spoiled, particularly the Duhallow,
Carbery and Muskerry regions.[37] Such destruction of the countryside
and inducement of famine conditions was a staple of warfare in
Tudor Ireland and became particularly acute in the closing years
of the Nine Years War. As a consequence the population of Ireland
fell considerably during the reign of Elizabeth I. Duhallow would
certainly not have been spared this and we can assume the region was
suffering from considerable demographic and economic damage by
the time James I ascended to the thrones of England and Ireland in
the spring of 1603. Indeed, writing four years later in 1607 the bishop
of Cork, Cloyne and Ross, William Lyon, stated that Munster was
still quite depopulated owing to the ravages of the war.[38] And yet this
brutal conclusion to the general crisis of Irish lordship in Duhallow
under the Tudors was not the end of the predicament that confronted
the Irish polities of north-west Cork. The advent of the Stuarts
saw Irish lordship in Duhallow enter a protracted period of internal
decline before its ultimate fall in the mid-seventeenth century.

5. The decline and fall of the Duhallow lordships, 1603–41

An intrepid traveller progressing through north Cork in the 1630s might well have arrived at a town on the edges of the region which, in the days of Elizabeth I, had been referred to as the impenetrable 'mountain of Sleulogher'. Our explorer would have entered a settlement of between two-dozen and thirty English houses. There were considerable signs of economic activity here, with an inn, a tannery and other shops visible on the main thoroughfare. Equally, goods would have been traded, primarily agricultural output from the farms that dotted the surrounding countryside. Dwarfing all the other buildings in the town was a castle, the residence of the Aldworth family, established there by the former provost marshal of Munster and vice president of the province, Richard Aldworth, who had died a few years earlier in 1629 and whose nephew and namesake, Sir Richard, was now the first citizen of this budding urban centre. Our traveller was in the town of Newmarket.[1] It had not existed twenty-five years earlier. The rapid development of this site, just a few kilometres from both Castlemacauliffe and Carrig Castle in the heart of the former MacAuliffe lordship, was the clearest illustration of the changes Duhallow experienced during the first half of the seventeenth century. At the close of the Nine Years War the barony retained virtually all of the political, demographic, social and economic hallmarks of its long history as a conglomeration of Irish lordships. Certainly the power of those same lordships had been immeasurably reduced by sixty years of increasing crown encroachments into Munster. But this earlier period might be said to have only constituted the crisis of Irish lordship in Duhallow. The years from the end of the Nine Years War through to the Confederate War of the 1640s saw the decline and fall of that system, as enormous transfers of land to English newcomers occurred and the political, social and demographic landscape of the region was irrevocably altered.

The decline and fall of the Duhallow lordships did not seem inevitable in the immediate aftermath of the Nine Years War. As elsewhere in Ireland the peace settlement arrived at for Munster by the new regime of James I in 1603 was remarkably lenient. In the north, for instance, Tyrone and his allies were pardoned. More broadly, an Act of Oblivion was passed, effectively pardoning anyone in Ireland who had taken up arms against the crown during the war.[2] The Duhallow lords, all of whom were implicated to varying degrees in the Munster insurrection, were now absolved of all wrongdoing. Art Óge O'Keeffe maintained his position in the south and west of Duhallow, as did Conor O'Callaghan to the east. The situation was more complex in Clanawley. Melaghlin MacAuliffe remained under crown custody beyond James's accession.[3] He most likely died a year or two later while still a prisoner.[4] His political successor in Clanawley in the years ahead was another Melaghlin, this one seemingly his grandson and a son of Dermot MacAuliffe who had been heavily involved on Tyrone's side during the Nine Years War and may have departed for Spain with his brother John in the aftermath of Kinsale.[5] Finally, while Donogh MacCormac's son Cormac was to attempt to continue to press his branch of the sept's claim to the MacDonogh lordship, there was little disputing that Dermot MacOwen was the preponderant power there in the post-war period. Remarkably, the man who had deigned to claim the Irish title of MacCarthy Mór just a few years earlier now found himself victorious in his twenty-year fight for pre-eminence among the MacDonoghs. In the years ahead he developed a grand new castle at Kanturk, a symbol of his confidence in his ascendancy, though one which, as we will see, inadvertently contributed to the rapid disintegration of the MacDonogh patrimony.[6]

Unwittingly, Duhallow became the object of one of early modern Ireland's most infamous pieces of jurisprudence in the first years of James's reign. In 1604 a dispute arose between Cahir O'Callaghan and Murrough MacBrian MacSweeney over possession of Dromaneen. The plaintiff, Murrough, claimed that the estate was his by right of the Irish practice of tanistry, or elective succession, while Cahir as defendant claimed it by right of English common law. The case was eventually referred to the higher court of king's bench in Dublin where, after a delay of several years, the attorney general of Ireland,

Sir John Davies, argued Cahir's side and with it the principal of English common-law inheritance trumping Irish succession through tanistry. Davies' law report on the case, published in 1615, has made the episode infamous.[7] Eventually in 1608 the plaintiff and the defendant settled out of court and agreed to split the Dromaneen estate, however the wider legal implications of the abortive case were profound. Discontent at the manner in which Irish succession laws through tanistry had been used as the basis for the claim, the senior judges in Ireland moved in the aftermath of the case to abolish tanistry in its entirety. The practice had been prohibited by implication in a ruling of 1606 on the custom of partible inheritance or gavelkind, but now in the aftermath of the O'Callaghan dispute a more firm ruling on tanistry was promulgated. As a result, in the early seventeenth century the small O'Callaghan lordship was front and centre in the decision of the Dublin legal establishment to effectively prohibit the custom of political succession within Ireland by tanistry.[8]

As much as the case of tanistry held the attention of officials in faraway Dublin, it was another development in landholding and legal authority in the early to mid-1610s that had the far greater bearing on early Stuart Duhallow. The reign of James I saw the eventual widespread introduction of 'surrender and regrant' schemes throughout north-west Cork. As we have seen in Chapter 3, these had been proposed for Duhallow as early as the 1570s. Conor O'Callaghan had subsequently entered into a limited arrangement of this kind in the mid-1590s. Now in the opening years of James's reign this approach came back into vogue. In the summer of 1604 the king ordered the government of George Carey to have an inquisition taken of Dermot's lands of Kanturk, Lohort and Castle Cor with a view to accepting a surrender of the same and regranting them to Dermot MacOwen.[9] This yet again proved abortive, as the old dispute between the two branches of the sept had re-arisen, with Donogh MacCormac's son, Cormac MacDonogh, pressing his suit against Dermot.[10] As a consequence in 1612 the long-serving viceroy, Arthur Chichester, was instructed to adjudicate on the matter and determine which of the two the crown should support as its preferred candidate for the lordship.[11] It took three more years for this to be resolved, but for Dermot this further wait must have seemed rather trivial given that he had been battling for preponderance at Kanturk now for over three decades. In the end he was victorious. In June 1615 Dermot MacOwen MacDonogh entered into a formal arrangement with the Stuart government whereby he surrendered his lands to James I. Two days later they were granted back to him in their entirety as the manor of Kanturk.[12] After thirty years of trying to establish himself as the head of the MacDonogh lordship, Dermot had finally solidified his position by becoming an English lord in central Duhallow.

He was not alone. In the early summer of 1611 Art Óge O'Keeffe had already been regranted his lands from the crown after he had surrendered them.[13] Within weeks of this covenant a similar bestowal had been made on Conor *na Cairrce* O'Callaghan, however in the lord of Pobble I Callaghan's case his power was diluted and the crown also entered into an agreement with Cahir O'Callaghan of Dromaneen whereby Conor received about two-thirds of the O'Callaghan lordship and his rival acquired the other third. At the same time, Brian MacOwen, head of the Duhallow MacSweeneys, received a regrant of his lands.[14] Therefore, between the summer of 1611 and the summer of 1615 all the major lords of Duhallow entered into a series of 'surrender and regrant' arrangements whereby they were finally reduced to the status of English landowners. These agreements transformed the nature of lordship in Duhallow. No longer were the land and power of the sept to be dispersed downwards to numerous other senior members and branches of the O'Callaghans, O'Keeffes and others. Rather, the 'surrender-and-regrant' arrangements of the 1610s saw the monopolization of power in the hands of Conor O'Callaghan, Art Óge O'Keeffe and Dermot MacOwen MacDonogh.[15] Only in the case of Cahir O'Callaghan was a collateral member of the sept provided with the kind of land grant which even vaguely reflected the diffuse nature of land distribution within these lordships during the sixteenth century. Thus, as Eve Campbell has demonstrated effectively in the case of the O'Callaghans, the septs' lands were wholly monopolized into the hands of just one or two members. By 1641 94 per cent of the remaining O'Callaghan lands were held by just two individuals.[16]

The arrangements were perhaps doubly necessary to shore up the position of these lords under James I, for the early Stuart period was seeing increasing calls for new plantations and land confiscation throughout Ireland. This was seen most spectacularly in west Ulster where, following the flight of the earls of Tyrone and Tyrconnell from Ireland in the autumn of 1607, an enormous plantation of the province from the Atlantic seaboard of Donegal all the way eastwards to the River Bann and Lough Neagh was undertaken. Other plantations followed in the 1610s, of Wexford, Longford and Leitrim, and many government officials were casting about for additional opportunities. For instance, in the autumn of 1612 the Irish solicitor general, Robert Jacob, composed a letter-tract in which he effectively proposed the extension of the plantation policy into virtually all those areas of Ireland still un-colonized.[17] Duhallow was not specifically mentioned, but Carbery in south-west Cork and several other nearby regions were. Equally, writing in the early 1620s the author of a series of 'Advertisements for Ireland' opined that 'Half of Munster and Ossory were never planted and are defective', the remedy surely being to finally extend the plantations into these areas.[18] There was then a very real danger from the early days of the reign of James I that much of Duhallow could be swallowed up by a cohort of avaricious newcomers.

These worries would not prove unfounded for very long and the early Stuart period witnessed the exponential growth in land speculation in the Duhallow region. In September 1607 Conor O'Callaghan mortgaged three whole ploughlands at Rathcoman and the surrounding region to Sir John FitzEdmond FitzGerald of Cloyne for £60. The temporary pawning of this considerable chunk of land was made permanent in 1620 when Rathcoman was sold to FitzGerald.[19] But it was Clanawley, with its oft-changing legal status, which unsurprisingly witnessed the first bout of land speculation on a grand scale. The exact status of the MacAuliffe lands in the aftermath of the Nine Years War is unclear, though it seems that they were still effectively in crown possession. Then in 1608 a shadowy land transaction was undertaken. This involved a triumvirate of adventurers, William Wakeman, James Carroll and James Hamilton, a trio who had been involved in other land speculation of dubious legality in Ireland in the 1600s. Through these transactions, Wakeman and his accomplices were profiting from acting as middle-men for controversial land dealings. Now sometime in early 1608 they acquired a crown grant of the entire Clanawley estate.[20] There the matter rested for over two years, until in December 1610 we find the triumvirate selling their recent gains to Thomas Roper, the constable of Castlemaine, just south of Tralee.[21] In the early 1600s Roper had developed a keen interest in the timber and pipe-stave trade in Munster. Duhallow, with its abundant and largely unexploited forests, must therefore have seemed an attractive prospect.[22] If this was his motive in entering into Clanawley his plans were quickly foiled as the government was simultaneously beginning a crackdown on rapacious timber-exporters in Ireland who were decimating the country's woodlands and exporting the produce to continental Europe. Consequently, Roper quickly set about leasing much of his newly acquired Clanawley lands to individuals such as Robert Bell, a New English newcomer from Norfolk. With Roper's acquisition of the Clanawley lands, then, the first concerted incursions of New English settlers into Duhallow began nearly three decades after the estate had first been confiscated by the crown.[23] Yet Roper's disinterest in developing Clanawley himself also provided an opportunity for Melaghlin MacAuliffe to reacquire a stake in his ancestral lands. In 1612 James FitzNicholas Barry of Walshestown near Churchtown purchased a large proportion of the Clanawley estate from Roper for £2,500 and immediately leased the same to Melaghlin MacAuliffe.[24] There were significant and long-standing close ties between the Barrys of Walshestown and the lords of Clanawley throughout the early modern period.[25] As such, James FitzNicholas' intervention at this time was an attempt to aid the MacAuliffes in resuming power in north-west Duhallow. However, the cost of this attempted restoration of Irish authority in Clanawley had been enormous, and in October 1612 Barry and MacAuliffe found themselves leasing a considerable stake in their lands to John Mayhew, a tenant who Roper had brought into the area.[26]

This circuitous transfer of lands in Clanawley in the late 1600s and early 1610s acquired greater cohesion in the mid-1610s. In 1614, disconcerted with the lack of profit accruing from the Duhallow lands, the government in Dublin established a commission to investigate how they might best be dispensed with to produce a profit for James I's coffers. In December 1614 an inquisition was held at Cork to explore these matters and how the lands could be let to produce an annual crown rental of £200.[27] One of the commissioners involved here was a certain Richard Aldworth. A son of an Englishman who had received an allotment on the Norris estate at Mallow in the late Elizabethan period, Aldworth was a member of the provincial council and in 1610 had become provost marshal of Munster.[28] Now, in late 1614, he took a personal interest in the Clanawley lands he had been involved in investigating. Thus, in the spring of 1615, having established that a portion of the Clanawley estate consisting of nine ploughlands, centred on the heartland of the former MacAuliffe lordship around *Áth Trasná* and Castlemacauliffe, should be deemed to be an estate worth £200 per annum to the crown, the commissioners induced James FitzNicholas Barry, Melaghlin MacAuliffe, Thomas Roper and various others to surrender all their interest in this section of Clanawley to the crown.[29] Subsequently, in December 1615 Aldworth was granted a crown lease of the nine ploughlands of *Áth Trasná* for twenty-one years, paying £200 annually for the same.[30] So began the long association of the Aldworths with the Newmarket region and the first concerted plantation of English settlers in early modern Duhallow.

The Aldworth plantation impacted considerably on the Clanawley region, particularly the area around the budding town of Newmarket. In the spring of 1616 the provost marshal applied for a renegotiated lease of the estate for sixty years.[31] In return he promised to establish a major English plantation at Newmarket, an offer which the Privy Council in England were particularly keen on, noting that 'those landes were most of them woode, bogg, mountaine and barraine groundes, lying in a remoate parte from the seates of any English, being the only passage betweene the counties of Corke and Kerrie, boundinge with either county' and 'were the meetest to be reduced and plainted with English of any parte of that province now unplanted'.[32] Consequently, in the summer of 1617 a fresh seventy-eight-year lease of the Newmarket estate was made to Aldworth, while in return he pledged to plant twenty families of English settlers at Newmarket within five years.[33] This he seems to have achieved. In May 1620 the town had developed sufficiently that a grant of the rights to hold markets and fairs there was made, and two years later in 1622 a market house was erected.[34] Although he died in 1629, Aldworth's nephew continued his work. By the end of the 1630s there were at least two dozen houses in Newmarket and the wider settlement would have been augmented by farmsteads in the surrounding region.[35] Thus, Richard Aldworth was the first figure to bring about radical transformation in Duhallow, and while Melaghlin MacAuliffe retained some of the lands he had acquired with James FitzNicholas Barry from Roper in 1612, the MacAuliffe presence in Clanawley was thereafter in terminal decline.

These encroachments into Clanawley were accompanied by several proposals to impose greater governmental oversight throughout Duhallow. In 1608 the lord president of Munster, Henry Danvers, suggested that Castlemacauliffe should be taken over and a crown ward established within it.[36] This scheme was never implemented, but another concerning the county structure of Cork itself was less transient. Proposals to divide county Cork into two smaller shires had been in the firmament during Elizabeth's reign. They abounded under James I. In 1606 Chichester's government in Dublin instructed the provincial administration of Munster to investigate a request by the citizens of Youghal to have a county of Youghal made out of their town and much of east Cork, with Duhallow forming a major part of a truncated county Cork formed out of the bulk of the west of the existing shire.[37] A similar proposal resurfaced at roughly the same time that Aldworth was acquiring his Clanawley lands, but again went little further.[38] Doubtlessly the most coherent proposal, though, and the one that would have impacted most substantially on Duhallow, was proffered by Aldworth himself. In June 1621 he wrote to the Privy Council to propose that a large chunk of Duhallow should be removed from county Cork and attached to county Kerry. He did not specify the exact area he envisaged as forming the new part of Kerry, but it was to include Newmarket where he also proposed that the circuit courts should periodically be held. Aldworth's proposal was given serious consideration, with discussion between the metropolitan government in London and the Dublin administration thereon throughout late 1621 and early 1622.[39] Although eventually rejected, it is indicative of increasing administrative shifts underway in north-west Cork at the time.

This administrative change, however, paled in its impact with the major development in Duhallow during the reigns of James I and Charles I. While the sixteenth century had seen a deep crisis of the Irish lordships there, little land had actually been lost by the Irish lords. That changed in the early seventeenth century as the financial situation of the MacDonoghs, O'Callaghans, O'Keeffes, MacQuirkes and MacSweeneys spiralled downwards. The undermining of traditional lordship in north-west Cork during the reign of Elizabeth I saw the economic power of the septs there weakening considerably by the 1580s and 1590s. Indeed, this phenomenon reflected developments throughout Ireland and much of the cause of the flight of the great lords of Ulster from Ireland in 1607 was owing to their dwindling economic fortunes. In the Duhallow instance the deteriorating state of the lordships was inadvertently hinted at by Aonghus O'Dalaigh in his poem *The Tribes of Ireland* penned around the turn of the century. Although written as a satire of the Irish lords, O'Dalaigh's depiction of the Duhallow chiefs as being impoverished and unable to provide adequate levels of hospitality was reflective of the dwindling economic position of the MacDonoghs, O'Keeffes, O'Callaghans and others throughout the region in the years ahead.[40] Above all, this economic decline led to the Duhallow lords mortgaging their lands to generate money to preserve their position. In doing so they set in train the process whereby an enormous transfer of land would occur by mid-century. This phenomenon began slowly in the early 1610s. For instance, in October 1614 Art Óge O'Keeffe mortgaged seven hundred acres of land at Knocknagree in Drumtarriff parish to a Cork merchant Stephen Meagh.[41] It was following the changeover of the heads of the lordships in the years that followed that the process escalated. After Conor *na Cairrce* O'Callaghan's death in 1612 he was succeeded by his relatively young son Callaghan MacConor, while Art Óge appears to have died in the 1610s and was followed as head of the O'Keeffes by his son Manus who would hold sway in Pobble O Keeffe down to the mid-1630s when his own son Daniel in turn succeeded him.[42] Dermot MacOwen lived until 1625, at which time his son and namesake inherited the MacDonogh lands.[43]

These new lords oversaw a massive increase in the scale of land mortgaging. In January 1620 Callaghan O'Callaghan aliened three-and-a-half ploughlands in Kilshannig parish and a further three-and-a-half in Clonmeen parish to James Lombard, a merchant from Cork city, whose family had longstanding interests in the region around Buttevant, and which was aggressively buying up land in Duhallow throughout the first half of the seventeenth century.[44] These acquisitions from O'Callaghan would form the basis of the estate that would be centred on modern-day Lombardstown some 10km west of Mallow along the River Blackwater.[45] In 1623 Callaghan sold two further ploughlands at Dromcomer in Clonmeen to another Cork-based merchant, William Terry.[46] Hence, much of the land being sold in Duhallow during the 1610s, 1620s and 1630s was acquired by a cohort of Old English merchant families from Cork city whose fortunes were thriving as early Stuart Munster enjoyed considerable economic development. In the 1630s others such as the Coppingers and Hores of Cork city and east Cork acquired lands from the O'Keeffes and others. These transactions also percolated downwards to the smaller septs within Duhallow.[47] In December 1628 Edmund MacSweeney and his son Brian sold approximately one thousand acres at Derrygallon between modern-day Boherbue and Kanturk to William Terry of Cork for £708.[48] In the mid-1630s the O'Mullanes of Brittas mortgaged the sept lands there to James Lombard for £700, though in this instance an arrangement was reached whereby the lands were immediately leased back to the O'Mullanes and this particular sept incredibly maintained a presence in their small enclave of Duhallow down to the 1820s.[49]

Yet these Cork merchant families were not the only ones acquiring land in Duhallow. Many others were New Englishmen. In 1631 Callaghan O'Callaghan mortgaged Monaveely in Kilshannig parish to the lord president of Munster, Sir William St Leger, for £115 as St Leger began to extend his interest from his core estate at Doneraile westwards into Duhallow.[50] But as the 1620s turned into the 1630s it was two individuals above all others who were acquiring substantial tracts of land throughout Duhallow. The first of these was Sir Philip Percival. Percival's father had been a clerk of the Irish Court of Wards in the early seventeenth century, a position which Philip acquired following his father's death in 1620. By employing the extensive funds that passed through his hands in executing this office, Percival was able to offer large sums of money to the major Duhallow landholders in return for mortgages of considerable tranches of their estates, a methodology he was also employing to acquire lands in Dublin, Tipperary and other parts of Cork.[51] None became more indebted to Percival than the MacDonoghs. Prior to his death in 1625 Dermot MacOwen had spent huge sums of money developing a grand castle at Kanturk, a project that was never finished, but the impressive

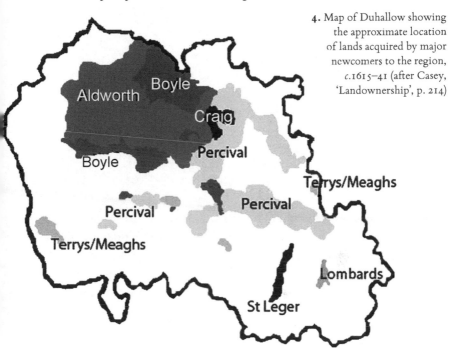

4. Map of Duhallow showing the approximate location of lands acquired by major newcomers to the region, *c*.1615–41 (after Casey, 'Landownership', p. 214)

remains of which attest today to his ambition. Yet, to undertake this grand project, Dermot had mortgaged vast tracts of land. Most strikingly, in the early 1620s he mortgaged and sold some 7,800 acres to Sir James Craig, a prominent Scottish courtier with extensive interests in Ireland.[52] His son and successor Dermot Óge continued this pattern and in 1627 mortgaged seven ploughlands at Clongeel and Ballyhowlahen in Kilmeen parish to Dominic Terry. From the early 1630s though it was Percival to whom MacDonogh turned most regularly for cash injections. In 1631 he mortgaged the castle, town and lands of Lohort and seven other ploughlands to Percival for £200, while a year later extensive lands at Cullen and Dromtarriff met the same fate for an additional £800. This figure gradually increased over the years that followed until Dermot was in hoc to Percival for approximately £2,400, an enormous sum that was well beyond MacDonogh's ability to repay. Having fatally compromised his own estate in this fashion, Dermot Óge began pressurizing the MacQuirkes, over whom he still held some residual authority, to further mortgage their own estates to Percival to fund his debts. Yet this paled in comparison with his own activities. By the time Dermot Óge died in 1635 over sixty ploughlands of the former MacDonogh lordship had been mortgaged to various parties for more than £6,000 in ready cash. Curiously Percival was directly involved in only about one-sixth of these lands, but he had loaned MacDonogh almost £3,000 himself and, by using middlemen such as Richard Osborne and John Webb, Percival's interest was in actuality much greater.[53] The stake he had acquired throughout Duhallow, largely on the MacDonogh estate, ultimately stretched to over 10,500 acres and the mortgages would subsequently allow his successor to take outright possession of these lands.[54]

Percival's acquisitive conduct in Duhallow in the late 1620s and 1630s was matched by only one individual, the first earl of Cork, Richard Boyle. Reputedly the wealthiest man in the three kingdoms, Cork had carved out a huge territorial empire centred on west Waterford and a vast stretch of Cork from Youghal west to the southernmost reaches of Ireland around Clonakilty and Baltimore. As he ran out of territory to acquire here, his focus switched further north and a huge expanse of land was acquired around Fermoy and further to the north-west in south county Limerick and north county Cork. At some point in the late 1620s and early 1630s he began expanding into Duhallow. Some of this comprised former lands of the O'Keeffes around Cullen, but most of it had been part of the MacAuliffe lordship in Clanawley. One large block was around Meelin in the northern extremity of Duhallow.[55] In 1632 Boyle also obtained the remainder of a twenty-one-year lease, which Percival had of Castlemacauliffe, while the earl acquired the castle, mill and lands of Carrig Castle from Simon Haly, a merchant from Kilmallock who had bought the same in the early 1630s.[56] Thus, Boyle was able to acquire these properties on the doorstep of Aldworth's Newmarket plantation. Finally, by 1636 the earl had come into possession of the rectory of Dromtarriff in Pobble O Keeffe and a large concentric block of lands in Kilmeen parish, specifically the townlands of Keelnahulla, Meens and Lisrobin extending from just north of present-day Boherbue towards Newmarket, while further acquisitions to the north-west at Knockaclarig extended the Boyle possessions to near Rockchapel.[57] Overall in the 1630s Boyle was able, through mortgages, leases and outright purchases, to acquire the bulk of those parts of Clanawley which had remained in the hands of Melaghlin MacAuliffe following Aldworth's acquisition of the Newmarket plantation lands.

While there is a considerable body of records extant in the government archives and those of the Boyles and Percivals with which to reconstruct the variegated manner in which land changed hands in early Stuart Duhallow, there is virtually zero evidence available through which one might assess the extent of the social, demographic, economic and cultural change that occurred in the area during the early seventeenth century. Limited as the evidence is, some assertions can be made. Clearly the biggest shift was in the arrival of large numbers of English settlers. The two central loci for this settlement were Aldworth's colony at Newmarket and the spill-over of English settlement into east Duhallow from what had been the Norris settlement at Mallow, and which from the early 1600s became the estate of John Jephson.[58] Yet this was not the scenario elsewhere. What evidence we have for the earl of Cork's lands at Meelin, for instance, indicate that he was continuing to largely lease his acquisitions there to Irish tenants.[59] Similarly, the lands acquired by Percival around Kanturk and elsewhere in the central corridor of the barony did not become the focus of extensive migration at this time. Unlike Aldworth at Newmarket, Percival was an absentee landholder, whose approach in the 1630s was to administer large tracts of land through his agent John Hodder and retain much of the original tenantry.[60] So too with many of the Duhallow lands acquired by the Cork merchant families of the Terrys, Meaghs and Lombards, the emphasis would have been on purchasing these lands as investments rather than allotments that were settled on by the new owners.

Despite these limitations on New English settlement, the impact of the migration into Duhallow during the first half of the seventeenth century on the society and culture of the region was significant. New urban centres emerged, most notably at Newmarket. English would have been spoken more frequently throughout the barony, though Irish would have remained the predominant tongue and bilingualism would have been necessary for many. Economic life changed in so far as the fairs and markets that came into being at Newmarket and elsewhere were more formal than their sixteenth-century Irish predecessors at Kanturk, Castlemacauliffe and Clonmeen. A few proto-industries would have appeared, though agriculture would remain the predominant basis of the economy, in many ways down to the twentieth century. Two tangible and dramatic changes in consumption though would have become noticeable with the introduction of tobacco and the potato from the New World, the former experiencing a huge consumer boom in the first half of the seventeenth century and the latter beginning to acquire its place as the staple food of the poor in Ireland by mid-century.[61] From a judicial and local governance perspective, the incursion of English government into the region which began in the sixteenth century advanced considerably and there is evidence of the principal Irish landholders among the O'Callaghans, O'Keeffes and others appealing to the local courts in Munster and the higher courts in Dublin. Equally, such individuals began to sit on juries on court cases in Cork city, while in 1613 Dermot MacOwen MacDonogh sat as an MP for Kanturk in the Irish parliament.[62] Finally, social interactions between the Irish of Duhallow and the English newcomers would have been considerable and after the initial disruptions of the 1610s and 1620s many began working together. No better sign of this is found than in the extensive correspondence between Conor Reagh O'Callaghan and Philip Percival, O'Callaghan having accepted a position as an agent of Percival's in the 1630s.[63]

There were also small indicators that the religious landscape was shifting. As elsewhere in Ireland outside of the towns the Protestant Reformation made virtually no headway in Duhallow during the sixteenth century.[64] The advent of the Stuarts saw a more concerted effort to ensure conformity to the state religion through prohibition of Catholic services and the imposition of fines on recusants who refused to attend state Protestant services.[65] Our information is pitifully small to determine the effect of these measures in Duhallow, but it was almost certainly insignificant in furthering the Protestant cause in this corner of Cork. In 1607 the bishop of Cork, Cloyne and Ross suggested that Duhallow was somewhat well provided for with Protestant preaching ministers.[66] The reports pursuant from the ecclesiastical visitation of Ireland in 1615 also provided some positive notes. Many churches in Duhallow were in a ruinous state, but a good many were also described as having been repaired and were served by

Protestant ministers, a situation that was better than that found during the ecclesiastical visitation of many other dioceses throughout Ireland in 1615 and again in 1622.[67] Yet the real state of the religious landscape was perhaps most truly attested to by Aldworth in 1628. Writing to the lord deputy, Henry Cary, Viscount Falkland, Aldworth claimed there had recently been a gathering of as many as two thousand people in a wood just 5km from Newmarket, headed by a dozen Catholic priests and some friars. One of the latter was a brother of Callaghan O'Callaghan, who had been overseas and had returned to preach near his brother's patrimony. The principal Irish landholders of the region had since been questioned, including Dermot Óge MacDonogh, but they had claimed that the meeting occurred spontaneously and was not planned, an explanation that Aldworth understandably suggested was improbable.[68] This gathering indicates the scale of religious non-conformity within Duhallow by the reign of Charles I and north-west Cork retained a staunch Catholic character going forward.

In closing his report, Aldworth had noted that the Irish of Duhallow were very poor. And that perhaps was the salient point. Protestantism, as the state religion, could not find traction among a native population that was increasingly impoverished through its interactions with that same state. By the end of the 1630s the economic position of the major Irish septs had deteriorated dramatically. The situation was most extreme in Clanawley where Melaghlin MacAuliffe and his successor Florence gradually lost most of those lands which they had reacquired with the aid of the Barrys from Roper in 1612, largely in gradual sales to Boyle. On the eve of the insurrection of 1641 Florence MacAuliffe retained just two thousand acres in north-west Duhallow. This was a pitiful holding for the senior member of a sept which at the outset of the reign of Elizabeth I had independently ruled much of north-western Duhallow.[69] The situation was little better for Cormac MacDonogh, a great-grandson of Dermot MacOwen and grandson of Dermot Óge, who became the head of the family shortly before the outbreak of the 1641 rebellion. His estate was wholly impeded through mortgages of vast swathes of land including the core territories at Kanturk and Lohort. Further to the south-west the O'Callaghan lordship was less encumbered. A marriage between the two branches of the sept which had split the bulk of the territory of Pobble I Callaghan in 1611 saw Donogh

O'Callaghan reunite the bulk of the remaining lands in the late 1630s.[70] This left him over half of the lands his ancestors had enjoyed during the sixteenth century, in large part because Cahir O'Callaghan had managed to avoid entering ruinous mortgages on the scale others had throughout Duhallow. Finally, to the west, Daniel O'Keeffe had succeeded his father Manus in the late 1630s. His patrimony had shrunk from a high of thirty-eight ploughlands as granted to Art Óge O'Keeffe in 1611 as part of his 'surrender and regrant' arrangement to just seven ploughlands less than thirty years later.[71]

Thus, by 1641 Duhallow, which had been one of the few regions in Munster to not experience any substantive land conveyances or plantation during the reign of Elizabeth I, had seen a huge transfer of territory to newcomers such as Aldworth, Boyle, Percival, James Craig, William St Leger and a cohort of Cork-based merchants such as the Meaghs, Lombards and Terrys. In total, James Casey estimates that over 20 per cent of the profitable land had changed hands, while this figure rocketed in the 1650s and 1660s as the more ruinous mortgages entered into by Dermot Óge MacDonogh and others were formalized into changes of ownership.[72] And it was not just at the top that this shift in land was occurring. As elsewhere in Ireland, the establishment of informal plantations such as Aldworth's at Newmarket would have served to push the Irish families who had been living around Castlemacauliffe and Carrig Castle onto poorer, more marginal lands. From there the path forward was one of gradual downward social mobility as the many O'Flynns, O'Connells, MacSweeneys and others who had held major allotments around sites such as these found themselves leasing smaller parcels of land. Families who had been smallholders during the Tudor period often would have lost their own allotments altogether and found themselves becoming landless labourers or cowherds employed by the newcomers. Such a pattern was repeating itself throughout parts of Ireland such as plantation Ulster during the first half of the seventeenth century and Duhallow would have fared little better.[73]

Despite all this, Duhallow would have retained a decidedly Irish character. The population was still predominantly Irish throughout the seventeenth century and, as such, Irish would have remained the dominant language. Irish cultural practices too still predominated. The process of anglicization would take much longer and would never be fully perfected, even by the nineteenth century. And yet the profound decline of Irish lordship in Duhallow was keenly felt. It was often reacted against. In the autumn of 1619 a proclamation was made at Cork against several members of the MacAuliffes, MacSweeneys and O'Shines for their rebellious activities in the region.[74] Their lawlessness must have been considerable and substantial rewards were offered for bringing them in to the government, dead or alive. Further pardons to Melaghlin MacAuliffe and a Ulick O'Keeffe in the early 1620s indicate continued unrest, while it is possible, though not clear, that Dermot MacOwen himself ended a long career in 1625 engaged in a local rebellion.[75] Clearly the arrival of many newcomers into Duhallow and the rapid shifting of lands as the lordships there entered a dramatic decline was arousing resentment that simmered and often boiled over in the latter stages of James's reign and into that of his son Charles. It would soon develop into something far more substantial and that climactic revolt would spell the ultimate fall of the Irish lordships of Duhallow.

Conclusion

On 23 October 1641 a carefully organized plot led by a number of disaffected Ulster lords was chaotically initiated and intended to overthrow the plantation in the north and simultaneously seize the seat of power in Dublin. Plans of the revolt had been discovered in the capital and so the rebellion was compromised from its very inception. Consequently, it lost its direction early on and what had been a coherently organized conspiracy led by figures such as Sir Phelim O'Neill and Conor Maguire, second baron of Enniskillen, quickly degenerated into a popular insurrection throughout Ulster, replete with attacks on and atrocities against the British planters in the north.[1] From Ulster the insurrection swept southwards in the winter of 1641. It is generally understood that it spread to south Munster belatedly, having first reared its head in Tipperary in late November 1641 and then spreading south-west into Cork, Limerick and beyond.[2] The experience of Duhallow, as subsequently attested to in the depositions made by the British settlers who had been living in and around Newmarket, suggests that the insurrection erupted in north-west Cork faster than in other parts of the county, as early as the first days of December 1641.[3] The colonists in Clanawley quickly made their way towards the town where the Aldworth castle offered some security. The cast of the insurgency indicated the extent of it. Florence MacAuliffe, the head of what remained of the MacAuliffe sept, was one of its leaders early on, as was Donogh O'Callaghan of Clonmeen. There were also numerous other MacAuliffes, O'Callaghans and MacDonoghs mentioned by the Newmarket settlers. Critically, many of the British settlers later deposed that those who joined the insurrection owed large sums of money to the residents of Newmarket and elsewhere, and it is tempting to speculate that the spiralling indebtedness of the Irish was a primary factor in many individuals' decisions to join the revolt.[4] Rebel activity became more concerted as December wound on and numerous settlers were attacked around Christmas Day 1641.[5]

Then early in January assaults were concentrated on Newmarket. On the night of 7 January the Aldworth castle, in which some two hundred settlers from Newmarket and the surrounding region had taken refuge, was seized by a rebel force led by Donogh MacDonogh of Lohort, Donogh O'Callaghan of Clonmeen, Donal O'Keeffe of Dromagh and Florence MacAuliffe of Carrig Castle. A handful of the settlers were killed including the tanner, Walter Bettrish, the town carpenter John Creagh, a glover Richard Augustine and a saddle-maker Edward Denny. Then the remainder were driven out of the castle and conveyed towards Mallow, during which journey many were stripped, either as a form of ritual humiliation or to uncover goods or money which they might be hiding.[6] Undoubtedly, the extension of the 1641 insurrection into Duhallow had laid bare the tensions that existed between the heads of the septs that, just a few generations earlier, had ruled Duhallow and those who had arrived since the early 1610s as part of the colonies of Aldworth and others.

Once the popular insurrection of the late autumn and winter of 1641/2 was over, the rebellion began to take on a more organized shape as a rebel government was established at Kilkenny. The war would last for over a decade as the vagaries of the wider English Civil Wars and Wars of the Three Kingdoms stalled efforts to supress the rebellion in Ireland. In Munster the conflict solidified into a struggle between a Confederate-dominated north and a Royalist-controlled south, as the Boyles and the provincial government focused on securing the major urban centres of Lismore, Tallow, Youghal, Cork, Bandonbridge and Kinsale. Consequently, Duhallow's geographical position on the frontier between these two zones of occupation became a major warfront. As a result, two pivotal engagements of the Confederate War, the Battle of Liscarroll in the early autumn of 1642, and the Battle of Knocknanuss in the early winter of 1647, were fought either in the barony or right on its doorstep.[7] The latter in particular, occurring in the heart of the former MacDonogh lordship less than 2km from Castle Cor, was a crushing defeat for the Confederate army and a harbinger of things to come for the Irish landholders of Duhallow who had revolted in late 1641.

The Confederate rebellion was crushed following the Cromwellian conquest of Ireland in the late 1640s and early 1650s. In its aftermath, the remaining Irish landholders of Duhallow were severely punished for their involvement in the long wars of the 1640s. Throughout Ireland, various interest groups received substantial land windfalls through the Cromwellian Land Settlement of the mid-1650s, the primary beneficiaries being the Adventurers for Irish Land who had funded the English parliament in the 1640s in return for promises of massive grants of land in Ireland once the country was reconquered, and the officers of the Cromwellian army who crushed the Confederacy from 1649 onwards.[8] The loss of many of the records appertaining to Duhallow of the Civil Survey and the so-called 'census' of Ireland carried out in the late 1650s limits our knowledge of these grants, but it is clear that the Cromwellian army command gained the bulk of the largesse in Duhallow. Roger Boyle, Lord Broghill, the third eldest son of the first earl of Cork and the one to whom the family lands in north Cork and south Limerick had been bequeathed, was, for instance, a substantial gainer around Clanawley. More lands were granted to those who had been in regiments under his command. One of these was Broghill's near subordinate, Sir William Fenton of Mitchelstown, while other captains under Fenton also acquired large grants of Duhallow land, notably Capt. Roger Brettridge who was bestowed with some two thousand acres at Castlemagner between Kanturk and Mallow, comprising the appropriated lands of Robert Magner.[9] Another Cromwellian army officer, Sir Peter Courthop, received seven hundred acres of O'Keeffe and O'Callaghan lands around Banteer.[10] The government surveyor and polymath, Sir William Petty, received well over a thousand acres of the core O'Callaghan lands around Clonmeen and Roskeen.[11] Sir Robert King, a son-in-law of Fenton's and the future first Lord Kingston, was granted much of the former O'Callaghan and O'Keeffe lands, particularly around Dromore and Pallas, as well as a significant tranche of the O'Noonan lands around Tullylease in the extreme north of the barony.[12] Finally, Sir Nicholas Purdon was the beneficiary of a significant estate to the east of Dromaneen not far from the eastern extremity of Duhallow near Mallow. These would subsequently pass to Sir John Longfield and formed the Longueville estate in the eighteenth century.[13]

A great proportion of these grants comprised lands that formerly made up parts of Pobble I Callaghan and Pobble O Keeffe. This was largely because these two lordships had the most land left available for confiscation in the 1650s. Clanawley had generally passed to the Aldworths and the Boyles prior to 1641, while Philip Percival's son and heir John Percival succeeded in the aftermath of the Confederate War in having the extensive lands throughout the MacDonogh lordship which his father had acquired in mortgage passed to him in perpetuity.[14] The availability of land in the south and east of the barony was further augmented by the departure of Daniel O'Keeffe to the Continent in 1652 and the decision to transplant Donogh O'Callaghan to county Clare and confiscate his Cork estate as part of the Cromwellian drive to force the Irish into the western parts of Ireland.[15] Consequently, by the end of the 1650s a vast transfer of the land in Duhallow which, prior to 1641, had remained in Irish hands had taken place. Some alterations to this occurred in the 1660s as the Restoration Land Settlement saw some of the Cromwellian grantees disenfranchised in favour of Royalist supporters of Charles I and his newly restored son, Charles II. Foremost here was Daniel O'Keeffe who was restored to a small, but not inconsequential, proportion of his lands at Dromagh. Although he died shortly thereafter, his son benefited from this rehabilitation. His grandson, another Daniel, retained them down to the end of the 1680s at which time he sided with James II in the Williamite War. When the O'Keeffe lands were granted away to the recently established Hollow Sword Blades Company in the 1690s it signalled the last major land confiscation from the descendants of the Irish lords who had controlled Duhallow at the inception of the Tudor conquest of Ireland in the mid-sixteenth century.[16] A number of MacAuliffes, O'Keeffes, O'Callaghans and MacDonoghs continued to occupy prominent positions within Irish regiments in the armies of the Catholic powers of continental Europe well into the eighteenth century, but virtually all traces of the Irish lordships to which they had belonged back in Duhallow had disappeared by the end of the seventeenth century.[17]

The new dispensation was dominated by the settlers who had acquired estates either side of the wars of the 1640s. Roger Boyle was elevated to the peerage as first earl of Orrery in 1660 and his descendants continued to control much of Clanawley into the eighteenth century.[18] The Aldworths were the major landholder in the Newmarket area down to the outbreak of the Irish Civil War in the early twentieth century.[19] The Percival presence was consolidated around Kanturk in Duhallow and further to the north at Liscarroll and Churchtown in the barony of Orrery and Kilmore in the latter part of the seventeenth century. Philip died young in 1647, but his son Sir John Percival became the first baronet Percival, while Sir Philip's great-grandson, John Percival, was in 1733 raised to the peerage as the first earl of Egmont.[20] The Percival family dominated the Kanturk region throughout the eighteenth and nineteenth centuries as it grew as a regional market centre. The King family continued to hold a substantial estate in Duhallow down to the mid-nineteenth century, while the influence of many of the other seventeenth-century newcomers to the region were enshrined in the emergence of major place-names such as Longueville and Lombardstown, which survive down to the present day. Ultimately, the landscape of Duhallow during the Ascendancy period was shaped by the developments of the seventeenth century.

In many ways, the story of early modern Duhallow is the story of the *other* Tudor conquest of Ireland. Regions such as the midlands lordships of the O'Connors and O'Mores in the mid-sixteenth century and the lands of the O'Neills in Ulster in the early seventeenth century were largely extinguished by the more well-known method of military conquest followed shortly thereafter by a state-sponsored plantation. By way of contrast, Gaelic Duhallow, like many other Irish lordships during the early modern period, was reduced much more slowly over a period of decades through a combination of crown administrative encroachments in the form of garrisons and taxation; the increasing economic impoverishment of the principal Irish landholders; the subsequent mortgaging and sale of lands to New English land speculators; and then the inexorable downward social mobility of the Irish nobility and gentry of the region. When all of this had made their situation precarious or then perilous the lords there joined the major revolts of 1598, 1641 and 1688. These all failed and each incrementally destroyed the remaining vestiges of land and power they possessed in north-west Cork. As such, the Tudor period witnessed a prolonged crisis of Irish lordship on the edges of Sliabh Luachra, while the decline and fall of those same polities inexorably followed in the course of the seventeenth century.

And what of 'the mountain of Sleulogher' itself, that vague agglomeration of mountain, bog and woodland in the west of the barony, which so many Tudor commentators had deemed impassable? It took until the nineteenth century for it to be fully overcome. In the 1830s the government initiated an experimental drainage scheme in western Duhallow. This was carried out on part of a nine-thousand-acre plot that had been confiscated from Daniel O'Keeffe in the 1640s, which was still in crown possession and which incredibly was still being referred to as Pobble O Keeffe. Overseen by Sir Richard Griffiths, better known for the famous valuation of Ireland he conducted from the late 1840s onwards, the experiment saw the western extremities of Duhallow finally made habitable. With the establishment of Kingwilliamstown (later renamed Ballydesmond) as a model town on the border between Duhallow and Kerry in the 1830s, the conquest of Duhallow, both geographically and politically, might finally be said to have been complete.[21]

Notes

ABBREVIATIONS

AFM	John O'Donovan (ed.), *Annals of the kingdom of Ireland by the Four Masters*, 7 vols (Dublin, 1851)
AH	*Analecta Hibernica*
APC	*Acts of the Privy Council of England, 1542–1631*, 46 vols (1890–1964)
BL	British Library
Cal. Carew MSS	J.S. Brewer et al., *Calendar of the Carew Manuscripts, 1515–1624*, 6 vols (London, 1867–1873)
Casey, 'Landownership'	James Casey, 'Landownership in north Cork, 1584–1641' (PhD, UCC, 1988)
CBM	Margaret Curtis Clayton (ed.), *The council book for the province of Munster, c.1599–1649* (Dublin, 2008)
CPRI	James Morrin (ed.), *Calendar of the patent and close rolls of chancery in Ireland, Henry VIII–Elizabeth*, 3 vols (Dublin, 1861–3)
CSPI	H.C. Hamilton et al. (eds), *Calendar of state papers, Ireland, 1509–1670*, 24 vols (1860–1912)
DIB	*Dictionary of Irish biography*
ed./eds	editor/editors
EHR	*English Historical Review*
fo./fos	folio/folios
Fiants	Kenneth Nicholls (ed.), *The Irish fiants of the Tudor sovereigns, during the reigns of Henry VIII, Edward VI, Philip and Mary and Elizabeth I*, 4 vols (Dublin, 1994)
HMC	Historical Manuscripts Commission
IHS	*Irish Historical Studies*
IPRJ	*Irish patent rolls of James I* (Dublin, c.1830)
JCHAS	*Journal of the Cork Historical and Archaeological Society*
JRSAI	*Journal of the Royal Society of Antiquaries of Ireland*
LPL	Lambeth Palace Library
MS/MSS	manuscript/manuscripts
NLI	National Library of Ireland
no./nos	number/numbers
NUIG	National University of Ireland, Galway
ODNB	*Oxford dictionary of national biography*
PRIA	*Proceedings of the Royal Irish Academy*
RIA	Royal Irish Academy
s.a.	*sub anno* (under the year)
SP	state papers
TCD	Trinity College Dublin
TNA	The National Archives of the United Kingdom
UCC	University College Cork
vol./vols	volume/volumes

INTRODUCTION

1 *Cal. Carew MSS*, ii, no. 349.
2 Ibid., iii, no. 441.

3 Samuel McCarthy, *The MacCarthys of Munster: the story of a great Irish sept* (Dundalk, 1922); William Butler, 'The

lordship of MacCarthy Mór', *JRSAI*, 5th ser., 36:4 (Dec. 1906), pp 349–67; idem, 'The lordship of MacCarthy Mór (continued)', *JRSAI*, 5th ser., 37:1 (Mar. 1907), pp 1–23; idem, *Gleanings from Irish history* (Dublin, 1925).

4 Herbert Webb Gillman, 'Pedigree of O'Callaghans, chieftains of Pobul-I-Callaghan, County Cork, from Cahir O'Callaghan downwards to 1650', *JCHAS*, 3 (1897), pp 201–20.

5 Con Tarrant, 'The chieftains of Pobul Uí Cheallacháin, Co. Cork', *Seanchas Dúthalla*, 5 (1984), pp 19–27; Joseph O'Callaghan, 'The O'Callaghans of Kilcranathan, County Cork', *JCHAS*, 92 (1987), pp 106–12; Eve Campbell, '*Pobul Uí Cheallacháin*: landscape and power in an early modern Gaelic lordship', *Landscapes*, 18:1 (June 2017), pp 19–36; idem, 'Displacement and relocation in early modern Ireland: studies of transplantation settlement in Connacht and Clare' (PhD, NUIG, 2012), pp 88–141.

6 Michael MacCarthy-Morrogh, *The Munster Plantation: English migration to southern Ireland, 1583–1641* (Oxford, 1986), pp 164–7. Also, see Nicholas Canny, *Making Ireland British, 1580–1650* (Oxford, 2001), pp 328–9.

7 Casey, 'Landownership', pp 153–216.

I. DUHALLOW IN TUDOR TIMES

1 Butler, 'MacCarthy Mór (continued)', p. 12; http://downsurvey.tcd.ie/downsurvey-maps.php#bm=Duhallo&c=Cork [accessed 23 June 2020].

2 Laurence McCorristine, *The revolt of Silken Thomas: a challenge to Henry VIII* (Dublin, 1987).

3 Casey, 'Landownership', pp 171–4; McCarthy, *MacCarthys*, pp 251–64; William Dennehy, 'The lords of Ella: the MacDonoghs of Duhallow', *JCHAS*, 3 (1894), pp 157–62.

4 *CPRI*, ii, pp 260–2.

5 Casey, 'Landownership', p. 164; *CPRI*, ii, pp 260–2; Kenneth Nicholls, 'The development of lordship in County Cork, 1300–1600' in Patrick O'Flanagan and Cornelius Buttimer (eds), *Cork: history and society* (Dublin, 1993), pp 157–211 at p. 158. Many of these details are derived from a tract by the grantee of

the Castleisland seignory in the Munster Plantation, William Herbert (TNA, SP 63/135/58); Co. Cork inquisitions, RIA, OS EI 20, 133.

6 Kenneth Nicholls, *Gaelic and Gaelicised Ireland in the Middle Ages* (2nd ed., Dublin, 2003), pp 189–90.

7 *Fiants*, Eliz. I, no. 5714.

8 M. van den Broecke, *Ortelius atlas maps: an illustrated guide* (Amsterdam, 1996).

9 Philip Lee, 'Notes on some castles of mid-Cork', *JCHAS*, 16 (1910), pp 128–31; 20 (1914), pp 57–68, 113–24 at pp 121–4.

10 Casey, 'Landownership', pp 200–1; D. Allen, *Ath Trasna: a history of Newmarket, County Cork* (Cork, 1973), pp 19–24.

11 Casey, 'Landownership', pp 209–10.

12 John D'Alton, *Illustrations, historical and genealogical, of King James's Irish army list (1689)* (Dublin, 1855), pp 839–44.

13 Lee, 'Notes', pp 63–7.

14 Nicholls, 'Development', p. 165.

15 Casey, 'Landownership', p. 201; Co. Cork inquisitions, RIA, OS EI 22, 193–5.

16 O'Callaghan, 'The O'Callaghans'.

17 Jean MacCarthy, 'The ancient and noble families of Duhallow', *Seanchas Dúthalla*, 10 (1996), pp 62–73 at p. 66.

18 O'Callaghan, 'The O'Callaghans', p. 106.

19 On Dromaneen, see Campbell, 'Displacement', pp 106–21. Also see James White Grover, 'Historical and topographical notes etc., on Buttevant, Doneraile, Mallow and places in their vicinity, volume 3', *JCHAS*, 19–22 (1913–16), pp 1–353 at pp 61–71; idem, 'Historical and topographical notes etc., on Buttevant, Doneraile, Mallow and places in their vicinity, volume 2', *JCHAS*, 17–19 (1911–13), pp 1–296 at pp 218–38.

20 Campbell, '*Pobul Uí Cheallacháin*', pp 27–9.

21 Kenneth Nicholls, *Land, law and society in sixteenth-century Ireland* (Cork, 1976), pp 17–18.

22 Casey, 'Landownership', pp 154, 212–13.

23 John Collins, 'The maternal ancestry of Daniel O'Connell: the O'Mullanes of Brittas and Whitechurch, Co. Cork', *JCHAS*, 54:180 (1949), pp 84–7; NAI, Ferguson MS 7, fo. 390.

24 William Reeves, 'St Beretchert of Tullylease', *Ulster Journal of Archaeology*, 6 (1858), pp 267–75; Paul MacCotter and Kenneth Nicholls (eds), *The Pipe Roll of Cloyne* (Midleton, 1996), pp 202–5.

25 Casey, 'Landownership', pp 155–6; MacCotter and Nicholls (eds), *Pipe Roll*, pp 210–12; Thomas Magner, 'The Magners of the Blackwater Valley, Cork', *Seanchas Dúthalla*, 6 (1986), pp 44–6.

26 David Heffernan (ed.), *Reform treatises on Tudor Ireland, 1537–1599* (Dublin, 2016), p. 23.

27 Ibid., p. 120.

28 Daniel MacCarthy (ed.), *The life and letters of Florence MacCarthy Reagh* (London, 1867), p. 9.

29 *AFM, s.a.* 1535.

30 The exception is Campbell, 'Displacement', pp 123–5, which looks at non-elite settlement in the O'Callaghan lordship.

31 Fiona FitzSimons, 'Tudor fiants', *History Ireland*, 23:4 (July/August 2015), p. 25.

32 *Fiants*, Eliz. I, no. 6558.

33 Ibid., no. 6566.

34 Grover, 'Historical … volume 2', pp 63–82.

35 *Fiants*, Eliz. I, nos 2928, 6762; Diarmuid Ó Murchadha, *Family names of County Cork* (Dublin, 1985), pp 153–5; James White Grover, 'Historical and topographical notes etc., on Buttevant, Doneraile, Mallow and places in their vicinity, volume 4', *JCHAS*, 22–8 (1916–22), pp 1–331 at p. 58 notes further O'Flynns at Longueville.

36 *Fiants*, Eliz. I, nos 2251–2, 2257.

37 The townland name 'Gneeves' is found in the parishes of Kilmeen, Castlemagner and Kilshannig. See www.logainm.ie/en/s?txt=Gneeves&str=on [accessed 26 June 2020].

38 Campbell, 'Pobul Uí Cheallacháin', pp 22–3.

39 Ibid., p. 23.

40 Alexander Grosart (ed.), *The Lismore Papers*, 2 series, 10 vols (London, 1886–8), 2nd ser., 1, pp 4–7, 112–15.

41 *Fiants*, Eliz. I, nos 2251–2, 2257, 2261, 6505.

42 Ibid., no. 2257.

43 Campbell, 'Pobul Uí Cheallacháin', p. 28.

44 Ibid.

45 *Fiants*, Eliz. I, no. 2251; MacCarthy, 'Ancient and noble families', pp 65–6.

46 Casey, 'Landownership', pp 158–9; Edward MacLysaght, 'Longfield Papers', *AH*, 15 (1944), pp 135–42 at p. 137; Ó Murchadha, *Family names*, p. 298.

47 Campbell, 'Pobul Uí Cheallacháin', pp 32–3.

48 Gerard Farrell, *The 'mere Irish' and the colonisation of Ulster, 1570–1641*. (Cambridge, 2017), pp 158–70.

49 David Heffernan (ed.), 'Six tracts on "coign and livery", *c*.1568–78', *AH*, 45 (2014), pp 1–33; Nicholls, *Gaelic*, pp 223–6.

50 Nicholls, *Land*, p. 11.

51 McCarthy, *MacCarthys*, pp 251–64.

52 *AFM, s.a.* 1510; William Hennessy (ed.), *The Annals of Loch Cé*, 2 vols (London, 1871), *s.a.* 1510.

53 *AFM, s.a.* 1524.

54 David Edwards, 'The escalation of violence in sixteenth-century Ireland' in David Edwards, Padraig Lenihan and Clodagh Tait (eds), *Age of atrocity: violence and political conflict in early modern Ireland* (Dublin, 2007), pp 34–78.

2. DUHALLOW AND THE RE-EMERGENCE OF CROWN POWER IN TUDOR MUNSTER, *c*.1534–79

1 McCorristine, *Revolt of Silken Thomas*.

2 Dean White, 'The reign of Edward VI in Ireland: some political, social and economic aspects', *IHS*, 14:55 (Mar. 1965), pp 197–211; Nicholas Canny, *The Elizabethan conquest of Ireland: a pattern established, 1565–76* (Hassocks, 1976); David Heffernan, 'The reduction of Leinster and the origins of the Tudor conquest of Ireland, *c*.1534–1546', *IHS*, 40:157 (May 2016), pp 1–22; Edwards, 'Escalation'.

3 Art Cosgrove, 'The execution of the earl of Desmond, 1468', *Journal of the Kerry Archaeological and Historical Society*, 8 (1975), pp 11–27; Anthony McCormack, *The earldom of Desmond, 1463–1583: the decline and crisis of a feudal lordship* (Dublin, 2005), pp 58–74.

4 *State Papers during the reign of Henry the Eighth*, 11 vols (1830–52), iii, no. 282.

5 *AFM, s.a.* 1583; Casey, 'Landownership', pp 209–16; Richard Cronnelly, *Irish*

family history (Dublin, 1864), p. 199; Albert Casey et al., *O'Kief, Coshe Mang, Slieve Lougher and Upper Blackwater in Ireland*, 10 vols (Birmingham, AL, 1952–71), i, p. xvii.

6 Cronnelly, *History*, p. 200; *CSPI, 1611–14*, no. 536; Casey, 'Landownership', pp 210–11 notes he was still probably mortgaging lands in the mid-1610s and may have lived to the end of the decade.

7 *AFM, s.a.* 1577; Casey, 'Landownership', pp 186, 192; O'Callaghan, 'The O'Callaghans', pp 109–10; Ó Murchadha, *Family names*, p. 67.

8 Ibid.; *Deacair comhaireamh a chreach*, RIA, 645 (24/5/27), p. 266.

9 *AFM, s.a.* 1578.

10 Casey, 'Landownership', p. 193.

11 The possibility that Melaghlin's was a lengthy rule is suggested in a letter-tract that Henry Sidney composed in 1576 in which he notes that the MacAuliffe lord was unable to attend a meeting of the lords of south Munster in Cork 'by Reason of extreme Age and Infirmitie': see Arthur Collins (ed.), *Letters and memorials of state*, 2 vols (London, 1746), i, p. 91. Donogh MacTeige O'Callaghan was also unable to attend Sidney owing to alleged infirmity.

12 Casey, 'Landownership', p. 171; McCarthy, *MacCarthys*, pp 252–3.

13 James Buckley (ed.), 'Munster in AD1597', *JCHAS*, 12 (1906), pp 53–68, esp. pp 67–8; Casey, 'Landownership', pp 171–2.

14 LPL, Carew MS 599, p. 206.

15 McCormack, *Earldom*, p. 70.

16 *State Papers during the reign of Henry the Eighth*, iii, no. 282; TNA, SP 60/8/39; Richard Bagwell, *Ireland under the Tudors*, 3 vols (Dublin, 1885–90), i, pp 241–2.

17 McCormack, *Earldom*, p. 71.

18 *DIB*, 'St Leger, Anthony'.

19 Brendan Bradshaw, *The Irish constitutional revolution of the sixteenth century* (Cambridge, 1979), pp 189–288; William Butler, 'The policy of surrender and regrant', *JRSAI*, 6th ser., 3:1–2 (Mar.–June 1913), pp 47–65, 99–128; David Heffernan, *Debating Tudor policy in sixteenth-century Ireland: 'reform' treatises and political discourse* (Manchester, 2018), pp 45–54.

20 McCormack, *Earldom*, p. 78.

21 *Cal. Carew MSS*, i, no. 172.

22 For a sense of this across the period, see Ciaran Brady, *The chief governors: the rise and fall of reform government in Tudor Ireland, 1536–1588* (Cambridge, 1994).

23 Canny, *Elizabethan conquest*; Dennis Kennedy, 'The presidency of Munster under Elizabeth and James I' (MA, UCC, 1973).

24 Heffernan, *Debating*, pp 61–2.

25 *State Papers during the reign of Henry the Eighth*, iii, no. 448.

26 White, 'Edward VI'; Edwards, 'Escalation'.

27 TNA, SP 61/2/12.

28 Heffernan (ed.), 'Reform', pp 7–15.

29 TNA, SP 63/23/5; Bagwell, *Ireland under the Tudors*, ii, pp 135–7; David Heffernan (ed.), 'An early Elizabethan treatise on Laois and Offaly', *Ossory, Laois and Leinster*, 6 (2016), pp 1–16.

30 Samuel Hayman, 'Unpublished Geraldine documents', *Journal of the Historical and Archaeological Association of Ireland*, 3rd ser., 1:2 (1869), pp 356–416 at pp 395–6, which presents transcriptions of TNA, SP 63/12/30–31.

31 McCormack, *Earldom*, pp 99–102; David Edwards, *The Ormond lordship in County Kilkenny, 1515–1642* (Dublin, 2003), pp 186–8.

32 TNA, SP 63/25/70(v–vi); *AFM, s.a.* 1568 gives a notice of Teige Roe O'Callaghan as being killed at the battle, however this is inaccurate.

33 TNA, SP 63/26/4(ix).

34 Canny, *Elizabethan conquest*, p. 68; *ODNB*, 'Carew, Peter'; Brady, *Chief governors*, pp 278–9.

35 TNA, SP 63/33/53.

36 Canny, *Elizabethan conquest*.

37 TNA, SP 63/28/2; Peter Piveronus, 'Sir Warham St Leger and the first Munster plantation, 1568–69', *Éire-Ireland*, 14:2 (summer 1979), pp 15–36.

38 TNA, SP 63/28/3.

39 *DIB*, 'FitzGerald, James fitz Maurice'.

40 C.R. Sasso, 'The Desmond rebellions, 1569–1573 and 1579–1583' (PhD, Loyola, Chicago, 1980), pp 98–178; McCormack, *Earldom*, pp 109–25.

41 TNA, SP 63/27/23; Heffernan (ed.), 'Reform', p. 64.

42 Ciaran Brady (ed.), *A viceroy's vindication?: Sir Henry Sidney's memoir of service in Ireland, 1556–78* (Cork, 2002), p. 63.
43 TNA, SP 63/28/38; TNA, SP 63/29/2, 5; Butler, *Gleanings*, p. 83.
44 TNA, SP 63/29/70; Brady (ed.), *Vindication?*, p. 70.
45 Ibid.
46 TNA, SP 63/39/62.
47 Thomas Johnson Westropp, 'The ancient castles of the county of Limerick (western baronies)', *PRIA*, 26C (1906/7), pp 201–64 at pp 237–8.
48 David Edwards (ed.), *Campaign journals of the Elizabethan Irish wars* (Dublin, 2014), pp 17–20; TNA, SP 63/29/86.
49 TNA, SP 63/34/4(i).
50 *Fiants*, Eliz. I, nos 2246, 2248, 2252.
51 *ODNB*, 'Perrot, John'.
52 Heffernan (ed.), *'Reform'*, p. 141.
53 Ibid., p. 143.
54 Ibid., p. 124.
55 *Cal. Carew MSS*, no. 266, p. 391.
56 Mary Ann Lyons, *Franco-Irish relations, 1500–1610: politics, migration and trade* (Woodbridge, 2003), pp 139–56.
57 *Cal. Carew MSS*, no. 293 (iii–iv).
58 David Edwards, 'Geraldine endgame: reassessing the origins of the Desmond rebellion, 1573–9' in Peter Crooks and Seán Duffy (eds), *The Geraldines and medieval Ireland: the making of a myth* (Dublin, 2016), pp 341–78.
59 TNA, SP 63/46/56(i).
60 Arthur Collins (ed.), *Letters and memorials of state*, 2 vols (London, 1746), i, p. 91. Donogh MacTeige O'Callaghan's representative might have been his grandson, Callaghan O'Callaghan. His son Donough was deceased by 1575.
61 Ibid., pp 91–3; Brady, *Chief governors*, pp 141–58; Heffernan, *Debating*, pp 137–43.
62 Sasso, 'Desmond rebellions', pp 268–353; McCormack, *Earldom*, pp 145–92.

3. THE CRISIS OF LORDSHIP IN LATE ELIZABETHAN DUHALLOW, 1579–98
1 Edwards (ed.), *Campaign journals*, p. 92. In his 'Breviate' of these events, the area is referred to as being by the 'River of Rossacon', evidently a reference to the River Owenanare in the townland of Rossacon to the north-west of Kanturk.

2 Ibid.
3 Ibid., p. 94.
4 On the course of the rebellion, see Sasso, 'Desmond rebellions', pp 268–353; McCormack, *Earldom*, pp 145–92.
5 *Fiants*, Eliz. I, no. 2505.
6 Butler, *Gleanings*, p. 102; Allen, *Ath Trasna*, p. 25; Casey, 'Landownership', p. 202.
7 McCormack, *Earldom*, p. 166.
8 *Cal. Carew MSS*, ii, no. 229, p. 190; Edwards (ed.), *Campaign journals*, p. 41.
9 TNA, SP 63/70/64; TNA, SP 63/72/37; Edwards (ed.), *Campaign journals*, p. 74.
10 *Cal. Carew MSS*, ii, no. 395.
11 Edwards (ed.), *Campaign journals*, pp 96–7; *Cal. Carew MSS*, ii, no. 408 (ii), p. 265.
12 *ODNB*, 'Grey, Arthur'.
13 Heffernan (ed.), *'Reform'*, pp 188–9.
14 Ibid., pp 219–21.
15 TNA, SP 63/101/41; TNA, SP 63/100/9.
16 TNA, SP 63/95/59–60; TNA, SP 63/96/3 (iii); *AFM*, *s.a.* 1582, 1583.
17 *DIB*, 'FitzGerald, Gerald fitz James'.
18 TNA, SP 63/99/76.
19 TNA, SP 63/101/10; TNA, SP 63/105/25.
20 *DIB*, 'FitzGerald, Gerald fitz James'; McCormack, *Earldom*, pp 177–8.
21 Anthony McCormack, 'The social and economic consequences of the Desmond Rebellion of 1579–83', *IHS*, 34:133 (May 2004), pp 1–15; TNA, SP 63/91/41 (i).
22 TNA, SP 63/97/15 (ii).
23 *AFM*, *s.a.* 1583.
24 Butler, *Gleanings*, p. 102.
25 *APC*, xxiii, pp 23–4; Allen, *Ath Trasna*, pp 26–7.
26 *Fiants*, Eliz. I, no. 5714.
27 *Cal. Carew MSS*, ii, no. 627.
28 HMC, *Salisbury MSS*, iii, pp 4–7; Casey, 'Landownership', pp 172–4.
29 *Fiants*, Eliz. I, no. 4533.
30 *AFM*, *s.a.* 1585.
31 MacCarthy-Morrogh, *Munster Plantation*, pp 1–69; Canny, *Making*, pp 121–234; Heffernan, *Debating*, pp 175–82.
32 *Fiants*, Eliz. I, no. 4751.
33 TNA, SP 63/129/28.
34 *Fiants*, Eliz. I, no. 5586.
35 Ibid., nos 5043, 5313.
36 *DIB*, 'Norris, Thomas'; John S. Nolan, *Sir John Norreys and the Elizabethan military*

world (Exeter, 1997); Kennedy, 'The presidency of Munster'.

37 *APC*, xxii, p. 556.
38 TNA, SP 63/136/21; TNA, SP 63/137/29; TNA, SP 63/138/13.
39 MacCarthy (ed.), *Life and letters*, pp 42–3.
40 Ibid., pp 55–6; TNA, SP 63/140/14.
41 TNA, SP 63/140/5.
42 *Fiants*, Eliz. I, no. 5304.
43 TNA, SP 63/152/41, 45(i).
44 *APC*, xix, pp 316–7; Co. Cork inquisitions, RIA, OS EI 18, 32–8.
45 *APC*, xx, pp 240–1.
46 TNA, SP 63/157/23.
47 TNA, SP 63/158/17–21; APC, xxi, p. 310.
48 TNA, SP 63/160/23.
49 *APC*, xxii, pp 148–9.
50 TNA, SP 63/165/72–5; TNA, SP 63/167/5; *APC*, xxiii, pp 233–4.
51 *APC*, xvi, pp 146–7; xix, pp 316–17.
52 TNA, SP 63/66/29.
53 *CPRI*, ii, pp 254–5.
54 Ibid., p. 260.
55 Ibid., pp 260–2.
56 Ibid., pp 335–6; *Fiants*, Eliz. I, nos 5903, 5908.
57 Brady, *Chief governors*, pp 140–58; Heffernan, *Debating*, pp 136–43.
58 Collected together in LPL, Carew MS 631.
59 LPL, Carew MS 631, fos 69r–70r
60 *Fiants*, Eliz. I, no. 4722.
61 *APC*, xxiii, pp 23–4.
62 *IPRJ*, p. 283; Allen, *Ath Trasna*, pp 26–7.
63 For the authoritative account of the war, see James O'Neill, *The Nine Years War, 1593–1603: Tyrone, Mountjoy and the military revolution* (Dublin, 2016).
64 TNA, SP 63/173/90; *DIB*, 'MacCarthy Reagh, Florence'.
65 *Cal. Carew MSS*, iii, no. 264.

4. DUHALLOW AND THE NINE YEARS WAR, 1598–1603
1 O'Neill, *Nine Years War*, pp 72–8.
2 *DIB*, 'FitzGerald, James fitz Thomas'.
3 O'Neill, *Nine Years War*, pp 82–4; Anthony Sheehan, 'The overthrow of the plantation of Munster in October 1598', *Irish Sword*, 15:58 (1982), pp 11–22.
4 *Cal. Carew MSS*, iv, no. 80, p. 78, for instance, notes that Dermot MacOwen was eager to take up arms against the government long before the insurrection of 1598.
5 Co. Cork inquisitions, RIA, OS EI 18, 82–8.
6 TNA, SP 63/202(iii)/128; TNA, SP 63/213/27.
7 Sheehan, 'Overthrow', pp 16–17.
8 TNA, SP 63/202(iii)/117.
9 *Cal. Carew MSS*, iii, no. 302; TNA, SP 63/202(iii)/124.
10 TNA, SP 63/202(iii)/169.
11 TNA, SP 63/203/103.
12 O'Neill, *Nine Years War*, pp 85–98.
13 TNA, SP 63/205/148.
14 TNA, SP 63/205/201.
15 TNA, SP 63/206/59.
16 *DIB*, 'Carew, George'; Cyril Falls, *Mountjoy: Elizabethan general* (London, 1955), pp 119–208.
17 MacCarthy (ed.), *Life and letters*, pp 259–61.
18 TNA, SP 63/202(iii)/6; *Fiants*, Eliz. I, no. 6407; *CPRI*, ii, p. 563.
19 TNA, SP 63/202(iii)/18.
20 *Cal. Carew MSS*, iii, no. 456; TNA, SP 63/207(vi)/75.
21 TNA, SP 63/207(v)/110(i)(d–e).
22 Standish O'Grady (ed.), *Pacata Hibernia; or, A history of the wars in Ireland during the reign of Queen Elizabeth*, 2 vols (London, 1896), p. 114.
23 *Fiants*, Eliz. I, no. 6499.
24 Butler, *Gleanings*, p. 98. An inquisition taken at Cork in Aug. 1604 asserts that Donogh died on 4 Aug 1600, but this is incorrect given numerous pieces of evidence from late 1600 and early 1601 indicate that he was alive in Ulster during this time: see John Collins, 'Unpublished Cork inquisitions in the Royal Irish Academy', *JCHAS*, 65 (1960), pp 76–82, 127–9.
25 O'Grady (ed.), *Pacata Hibernia*, p. 161.
26 Allen, *Ath Trasna*, pp 28–9.
27 J. Silke, *Kinsale: the Spanish intervention in Ireland at the end of the Elizabethan wars* (New York, 1970); O'Neill, *Nine Years War*, pp 100–5; Hiram Morgan, *The Battle of Kinsale* (Wicklow, 2004).
28 *Cal. Carew MSS*, iv, nos 132, 229; John Maclean (ed.), 'Letters from Sir Robert Cecil to Sir George Carew', *Camden Society*, 88 (1864), p. 87.
29 He was still under restraint in the late spring of 1602: see *Cal. Carew MSS*, iv, no. 229; TNA, SP 63/211/7.

30　*Fiants*, Eliz. I, no. 6762.
31　*AFM*, *s.a.* 1601.
32　*Fiants*, Eliz. I, no. 6762.
33　Butler, *Gleanings*, p. 102.
34　*Cal. Carew MSS*, iv, nos 291–2.
35　Allen, *Ath Trasna*, p. 32; *CSPI, 1603–6*, no. 640; TNA, SP 63/223/80.
36　Vincent Carey, '"What pen can paint or tears atone?"': Mountjoy's scorched earth campaign' in Hiram Morgan (ed.), *The Battle of Kinsale* (Wicklow, 2004), pp 205–16; O'Neill, *Nine Years War*, pp 173–80.
37　*Cal. Carew MSS*, iv, nos 241, 291–2.
38　TNA, SP 63/221/35(a).

5. THE DECLINE AND FALL OF THE
DUHALLOW LORDSHIPS, 1603–41

1　MacCarthy-Morrogh, *Munster Plantation*, p. 165. Also see the 1641 depositions which reported on Newmarket in TCD MSS 823–826.
2　John McCavitt, *The flight of the earls* (Dublin, 2002).
3　*CBM*, pp 129–30.
4　Ó Murchadha, *Family names*, p. 10.
5　Butler, *Gleanings*, p. 102; *CSPI, 1603–6*, no. 640 lists a Dermot MacAuliffe in Spanish employ in 1606.
6　James Delle, '"A good and easy speculation": spatial conflict, collusion and resistance in late sixteenth-century Munster, Ireland', *International Journal of Historical Archaeology*, 3:1 (Mar. 1999), pp 11–35.
7　John Davies, *A report of cases and matters in law, resolved and adjudged in the king's courts in Ireland, collected and digested by Sir John Davies* (Dublin, 1762), pp 78–115.
8　Butler, *Gleanings*, pp 80–92; Hiram Morgan, 'Tanistry, Case of' in S. Connolly (ed.), *The Oxford companion to Irish history* (2nd ed., Oxford, 2002); *CBM*, pp 34–5, 43; Crawford, *Star chamber court*, pp 48, 156, 308–9; Casey, 'Landownership', pp 106–11.
9　*CSPI, 1603–6*, no. 300.
10　Bodleian Library, Carte MS 61, p. 146; *CSPI, 1608–10*, no. 897.
11　*CSPI, 1611–14*, no. 404.
12　*IPRJ*, p. 282.
13　Ibid., p. 207.
14　Ibid., pp 197, 200–1; *CSPI, 1608–10*, no. 966; *CSPI, 1611–14*, no. 536; Casey, 'Landownership', pp 190–1.

15　Butler, 'Surrender and regrant', pp 112, 125–7.
16　Campbell, '*Pobul Uí Cheallacháin*', pp 33–4.
17　Canny, *Making*, p. 176.
18　George O'Brien (ed.), *Advertisements for Ireland* (Dublin, 1923), p. 20.
19　John Ainsworth and Edward MacLysaght (eds), 'Survey of documents in private keeping, second series', *AH*, 20 (1958), pp 1–393 at p. 58.
20　Allen, *Ath Trasna*, p. 33; *IPRJ*, pp 283–4.
21　Ibid., pp 208, 283–6.
22　*CSPI, 1611–14*, no. 125.
23　Casey, 'Landownership', p. 204.
24　*IPRJ*, p. 284; Casey, 'Landownership', pp 163–4, 205; Allen, *Ath Trasna*, p. 35.
25　*Fiants*, Eliz. I, no. 2246; Grover, 'Historical … volume 4', pp 310–15; MacCotter and Nicholls (eds), *Pipe Roll*, pp 206–8.
26　*IPRJ*, pp 276, 285–6; Edward MacLysaght (ed.), *Calendar of the Orrery Papers* (Dublin, 1941), pp 280, 291–2; Casey, 'Landownership', p. 205.
27　*IPRJ*, pp 285–6.
28　Ibid., p. 173; *CBM*, p. 188; *CPRI*, iii, p. 211; MacCarthy-Morrogh, *Munster Plantation*, p. 165.
29　*IPRJ*, p. 284.
30　Ibid., pp 293–4, 300; Mary O'Dowd (ed.), '"Irish concealed lands papers" in the Hastings Manuscripts in the Huntington Library, San Marino, California', *AH*, 31 (1984), pp 69–192 at p. 157; Casey, 'Landownership', pp 205–6.
31　*APC*, xxxiv, p. 470; xxxviii, pp 146–7.
32　Ibid., p. 587.
33　*IPRJ*, p. 325; O'Dowd (ed.), '"Concealed lands papers"', pp 121–2.
34　Allen, *Ath Trasna*, p. 48.
35　MacCarthy-Morrogh, *Munster Plantation*, p. 165.
36　TNA, SP 63/224/143(i).
37　*CSPI, 1603–6*, no. 787.
38　*CBM*, pp 204–5.
39　Victor Treadwell (ed.), *The Irish Commission of 1622: an investigation of the Irish administration, 1615–22, and its consequences, 1623–24* (Dublin, 2006), pp 90–1; TNA, SP 63/236/6(b); *APC*, xxxviii, pp 146–7, 321–2.
40　John O'Donovan (ed.), *The tribes of Ireland* (Dublin, 1852), pp 66–9.

41 Casey, 'Landownership', p. 211.
42 Eddie Horgan, 'The O'Keeffes of Dromtariffe', *Seanchas Dúthalla*, 6 (1986), pp 52–3; Grover, 'Historical ... volume 3', p. 59.
43 Casey, 'Landownership', pp 181–2.
44 Ibid., pp 193–4.
45 Grover, 'Historical ... volume 4', pp 46–58.
46 Casey, 'Landownership', p. 194.
47 Ibid., pp 166–9, 214.
48 MacLysaght (ed.), 'Longfield papers', p. 137.
49 Casey, 'Landownership', p. 195.
50 Ibid., p. 196.
51 MacCarthy-Morrogh, *Munster Plantation*, pp 165–6; *DIB*, 'Percival, Phillip'; Sophia Crawford Lomas (ed.), *Report on the manuscripts of the Earl of Egmont*, 2 vols (London, 1905–9), i, pp viii–l; Canny, *Making*, pp 328–9.
52 Casey, 'Landownership', p. 180.
53 Ibid., pp 181–6.
54 BL, Add. MS 47,036; MS 47,039; MS 47,043; Lomas (ed.), *Report*, i, *passim*; Casey, 'Landownership', pp 381–5; MacCarthy-Morrogh, *Munster Plantation*, pp 165–7; Canny, *Making*, pp 328–9.
55 Casey, 'Landownership', p. 185; NLI, MS 6,142, p. 117.
56 Casey, 'Landownership', p. 208.
57 MacLysaght (ed.), *Orrery papers*, pp 81–3; NLI, MS 8,366, indicates these lands had been acquired by 1636. See Dorothea Townshend, *The life and letters of the great earl of Cork* (London, 1904), pp 472–3, for the relevant sections from Boyle's updated will in 1642.
58 Henry Berry, 'The English settlement in Mallow under the Jephson Family', *JCHAS*, 12 (1906), pp 1–26.
59 NLI, MS 6,142, p. 117.
60 MacCarthy-Morrogh, *Munster Plantation*, pp 166–7.
61 Toby Barnard, *The kingdom of Ireland, 1641–1760* (Basingstoke, 2004), p. 13.
62 Casey, 'Landownership', p. 179; TNA, SP 63/215/77(i); TNA, SP 63/236/33(b); Crawford, *Star chamber court*, pp 516–17.
63 Lomas (ed.), *Report*, i, pp 63–4.
64 Henry Jefferies, *The Irish church and the Tudor reformations* (Dublin, 2010).
65 John McCavitt, 'Lord Deputy Chichester and the government's

"mandates policy" in Ireland, 1605–7', *Recusant History*, 20 (1990), pp 320–35.
66 TNA, SP 63/221/35(a).
67 Michael Murphy, 'The royal visitation of Cork, Cloyne, Ross and the College of Youghal', *Archivium Hibernicum*, 2 (1913), pp 173–215; idem, 'The royal visitation, 1615 dioceses of Ardfert [and Aghadoe]', *Archivium Hibernicum*, 4 (1915), pp 178–98.
68 *CSPI, 1625–32*, no. 1057(i).
69 Butler, *Gleanings*, p. 102; Allen, *Ath Trasna*, pp 36–7.
70 Casey, 'Landownership', p. 199.
71 Ibid., p. 215.
72 Ibid., pp 215–16, 398.
73 Farrell, '*Mere Irish*', pp 153–214.
74 *CBM*, pp 212–13, 215–16.
75 Ibid., pp 221–6; Casey, 'Landownership', pp 181–2.

CONCLUSION

1 Michael Perceval-Maxwell, *The outbreak of the Irish rebellion of 1641* (London, 1994).
2 Canny, *Making*, pp 524–34.
3 See TCD MS 824, fos 66r–67v, where Thomas Grant claimed that he was assailed as early as 4 December 1641.
4 TCD MS 825, fos 20r–21v, 259r–260v.
5 TCD MS 823, fos 25r–26v; MS 826, fos 94r–94v.
6 TCD MS 825, fos 48r–49v.
7 Grover, 'Historical ... volume 3', pp 349–53.
8 David Brown, *Empire and enterprise: money, power and the adventurers for Irish land during the British civil wars* (Manchester, 2020).
9 Niall O'Brien, 'Roger Brettridge, the 1662 Act of Settlement and Duhallow affairs at the court of claims, 1663', *Seanchas Dúthalla*, 15 (2011), pp 10–17; Magner, 'The Magners'; Grover, 'Historical ... volume 2', p. 120.
10 Grover, 'Historical ... volume 1', p. 279.
11 Grover, 'Historical ... volume 2', p. 233; Grover, 'Historical ... volume 4', p. 185.
12 *DIB*, 'King, John'; Grover, 'Historical ... volume 4', pp 129–33, 151–2, 264.
13 Grover, 'Historical ... volume 4', p. 59.
14 Grover, 'Historical ... volume 3', p. 197.
15 Campbell, '*Pobul Uí Cheallacháin*'.
16 Horgan, 'The O'Keeffes'.
17 For instance, the ostensible head of the MacAuliffes left Ireland in 1691 and the

last direct chief of the sept died in Spain in 1720: see Allen, *Ath Trasna*, p. 45.

18 MacLysaght (ed.), *Orrery papers*, pp 23–5, 81–3, 280, 285; Patrick Little, *Lord Broghill and the Cromwellian union with*

Ireland and Scotland (Woodbridge, 2004).

19 Allen, *Ath Trasna*, pp 47–8.

20 *DIB*, 'Perceval, John'.

21 Casey, 'Landownership', p. 162; Cronnelly, *History*, p. 207.